A New Way To Look At Retirement

D0595282

First edition. Sixth printing.

ISBN-13: 978-0-9828887-7-3

This publication contains the opinions and ideas of the author. It is sold with the understanding that neither the author nor publisher is engaged in rendering legal, tax, investment, insurance, financial, accounting, or other professional advice or services. If a reader requires such advice or services, a competent professional should be consulted. References to organizations have been given for the purpose of information and do not constitute a recommendation. Any perceived slights of specific people or organizations are unintentional.

No warranty is made with respect to the accuracy or completeness of the information contained herein, and both the author and publisher specifically disclaim any responsibility for any liability, loss or risk, personal or otherwise, which is incurred as a consequence, directly or indirectly, by the use of any of the contents of this book. While the information and advice in this book are believed to be accurate and true at the time of publication, neither the author, publisher or distributor can guarantee results nor accept any responsibility or liability for any damage or losses of any kind resulting from any advice included in this guide, be it from the author, any person or persons mentioned in this book, or any product, listing or mention, whether directly or indirectly.

Table of Contents

About The Author – Ken Mahoney

An accomplished financial advisor, author, and speaker, Ken brings over 24 years of professional experience to residents of the New York City metropolitan area. Ken appears often on National TV. Ken is a guest financial contributor on CNBC and WPIX. He is also a financial analyst on Fox Business and Ebru TV.

He is the owner of Mahoney Asset Management. Ken's opinions on the world of finance have been published nationally. His expertise has not gone unnoticed by the periodicals either. Ken's market comments and perspectives are published in the Hudson Valley Business Weekly. His financial opinions have been published by USA Today, Investor's Business Daily, as well as by various local publications. He is a familiar quoted figure in the business pages of The Journal News and was a respected member of the newspaper's Business Leaders Roundtable. Ken hosted WRKL Radio's Smart Investor show from 1992 to 1998, and co-hosted Financial Mobility on WRKL and TKR. He also hosted Invest in You Community in the early 1990s. Since 1992, Ken has published the financial newsletter, The Smart Investor.

He is now on the Board of Richmond Community Services, on which he works to support people and their families with developmental disabilities. He is also the Co-Chair of the Business Council of the Make-A-Wish foundation, for which the goal is to raise funds to support the mission of granting wishes to children.

Ken also served for seven years as a member of the Board of Directors for Meals on Wheels and has been involved in the agency's golf and tennis challenge. Meals on Wheels honored Ken as Rockland's Community Leader of the Year in 2002.

He has earned distinguished service awards from the NY State Legislation, County of Rockland, and NY State Assembly for his work with charities. Ken Mahoney is the creator of the Westchester Stock Index and the Rockland Stock Index, both of which have appeared in a number of newspapers. The indexes are composed of local companies and are compared to national indexes.

Ken is also the author of Investing From Within: A Story of Understanding, which offers investment advice to various personality types. He also launched a series entitled The Zoo Exchange: Teaching Our Kids About Money, which teaches children about finance principles.

Ken's book, Now What? book focuses on protecting your capital, making tax efficient distributions, and transferring your wealth in the most economical way. His Now What? blog is updated frequently at http://kenmahoney.blogspot.com/.

His book, Can I Retire? has been a popular book for pre-retirees. Ken gives formulas and projections to answer the question, Can I Retire?   http://www.amazon.com/Retire-Your-Personal-Guide-Retirement/dp/0982888708

He now gives a market report every morning on WRCR 1300 am at 8:30 am www.wrcr.com and WTBQ 1110 am and 99.1 fm at 7:30, as well as WHUD 100.7 FM www.whud.com.

Ken is a Multiple Tony Award Winner and Grammy nominated Producer. His 'hits' include Pippin, Macbeth, Gershwin's Porgy and Bess (Best Revival of a Musical), and The Best Man (Best Revival of a Play). Ken shows in the 2011-2012 received a total of 14 Tony nominations. Ken is also the Executive Producer of the Cast Album's: Matilda, The Grinch, Jekyll and Hyde, 'How to Succeed in Business' with Nick Jonas, and 'Nice Work if you can get it' with Mathew Broderick. 'Nice Work if you can get it' was nominated for a Grammy. Ken also is the Executive Producer of live albums at 54 Below. His albums include Tony Winners Patti Lupone and Norbert Leo Butz.

Dedication

This book is dedicated to all my clients who have entrusted Mahoney Asset Management to help them plan for their futures. I also appreciate the friendships I have made with each and every one of them.

Special thanks to Susan Cataldo, Megan Kennedy, Gina Sundvik, Mary Maddren and Kenna DiBuono for helping to put this book together.

To my family, friends and colleagues, who continually inspire me, thanks for the words of wisdom!

I also dedicate this book to my mother who recently passed away.

The mission of Mahoney Asset Management
Know our clients well
Anticipate their needs
Exceed their expectations!!

Preface

'Age is an issue of mind over matter. If you don't mind, it doesn't matter.' ~ Mark Twain

There really is a new way to look at retirement.

When our parents' generation retired, they retired for good. They may have retired at 62 and passed away at 66. Today, we are living longer, healthier lives. Our parents and grandparents were also part of the manufacturing generation. They had to work very hard and the body could only last for so many years. Today, we have transitioned into a service economy where people can work much longer. It's not uncommon to see people work in their 80's and 90's. Now enter 'serial retirement' -- a name I came up with for those who have several retirements in their lifetime. The fact is, most retirees do not have a plan to go back to work, but after a year or so, some get itchy to do something.

I have seen retirees call it quits at 60, then at 62 go back to help a son's/daughter's business for a few years, retire again, a year later get involved in a small business and repeat. I have had clients retire 3 or 4 times with this 'serial retirement'.

I am not suggesting you have to do this, just be aware that many people are doing this now. However, their 2nd 'act' is something they love doing and happen to get paid for it.

A New Way To Look At Retirement

In my last book, "Can I Retire?" I talked about how a lot of people are still really unsure about *when* they can retire and what they need to make it happen. Most people spend a long time just being upset and worrying about the mere thought of retirement. Some people even told me they'd wake up in a sweat wondering whether they'll ever have enough money to support them through their retirement years. The only real answer to that question is a projection - working out your income in the future; looking at your assets and how you could draw income from those assets. (See "Projections" chapter at the end of this book).

Saving for retirement is one of the most important tasks you will undertake in your adult life. This book aims to help you achieve this goal by showing you how you can effectively work with your assets and make the most of your years before and after retirement.

While retirement used to be considered by many as the final stage of their lives, it's actually just the beginning of a new stage of your life. This new stage in life should bring fulfillment. Maybe it's time for you to travel to places that you've never before had the time or means to visit, or indulge in hobbies that were impossible to enjoy because of time restraints. (Please ask about our companion workbook that covers this topic in great detail).

Maybe you'll even think of it as an opportunity to spend longer hours with your family and friends. Most likely, though, it's a combination of all of these things.

What retirement should NOT be is a time for worrying about whether or not you can afford travelling to all those places you've always wanted to visit, enjoying that hobby you never had time for before, or worst of all, being unsure of whether or not you can afford to retire and live comfortably.

Whether we like to admit it or not, money is just as important during retirement as it is during your working life—maybe even more so actually, since you will no longer have a regular stream of income coming in from your job.

I'm not saying that your income is supposed to stop. On the contrary, by the time you finish reading this book you should have a clear-cut plan as to what you want to do with your life after retirement, including a plan to have various sources of income so that you can enjoy this stage of your life.

By planning ahead, you can ensure that you are financially able to have the lifestyle you want. By considering your goals and your potential financial resources, you'll be giving yourself the best possible chance of succeeding.

If you are one of the 76 million baby boomers who have recently retired, or soon will, the odds are good that your prime earning years are already behind you, or will be soon.

So now it's time to focus your financial planning on the distribution years.

A New Way To Look At Retirement

The best thing about having a well-thought out plan for your future is that it gives you the luxury of enjoying today and feeling secure that your retirement years are being provided for. *It's about being able to strike a balance between living for today and preparing for tomorrow.*

> *"The willingness and ability to live fully in the now eludes many people. While eating your appetizer, don't be concerned with dessert."* ~ Dr. Wayne Dyer

A recent study shows that people spend more time planning their own one-week vacation than they do planning for their retirement. Isn't that crazy? It's true! People spend more time planning vacations, getting on the Internet, browsing sites like Tripadvisor.com, speaking to/Facebooking their friends, really planning out a nice itinerary, places they want to see, restaurants they want to go to, sites they want to visit. Yet, they don't have the same enthusiasm when it comes to planning for retirement. Why? After all, what is retirement if not a very long vacation?

I think planning for your vacation is definitely a smart thing to do, having your days planned out and leaving some time out for spontaneity when it comes to a vacation. I haven't met anyone who doesn't enjoy planning their vacations, it's a fun activity.

Yet when it comes to retirement planning, people get the heebie jeebies. They don't want to sit down and plan it, or even think about it, because they are scared. Why not focus that same enthusiasm, that same excitement of planning a vacation on their retirement planning? I always tell people to start off by considering their destination. Okay, we want to go here, we want to go there; but how do we get there? So that's definitely the first question to answer.

While the retirement age used to begin at 40+, today most people retire at about 65. This book will help guide you not only in preparing NOW for your future of non-working bliss, but it will also show you how to keep yourself there once you ARE retired. If you're anything like most people on the brink of retirement today, you're already asking yourself whether or not you're ready for retirement. When I say ready, I mean financially. You could very well have enough money to retire now and don't realize it yet; or, on the other hand, you may be ready for retirement mentally but come to the conclusion that you don't have enough money; or you aren't even sure how much money you will need to retire comfortably.

This book will help you determine where you are currently, how you can prepare for your retirement, and what measures you can take to ensure that you are secured financially and prepared mentally for the big transition!

Believe it or not, you probably have more assets than you think. With the right planning, you can make your assets last longer than many believe possible. You will see how the same compound interest that worked against you when you were paying off your mortgage and credit card bills, will now help to keep your investments growing as the years in life rush by, even as you make regular withdrawals.

A New Way To Look At Retirement

Whether you've dreamed and planned for this new phase of life or you've dreaded the day and judiciously avoided the planning you knew you should have been doing, today really is the first day of the rest of your life. Retirement is a whole new ballgame, so you better learn the rules so you can play to win.

Even though what the future holds is unknown, you can make reasonable predictions about how it will likely affect your health and financial situation. You can choose to take steps now, and during other key times, that will make your retirement years relatively stress-free. Or you can choose the "Que Sera, Sera" path and wait to see what happens. Unfortunately, the likely outcome of not planning and thinking these issues through is … well, I'd rather not say. It's too daunting!

In this book, I'm going to focus more on investment strategies and ways that you can continue to make money that will equip you with the necessary tools to make your retirement possible. It doesn't matter how much or how little you know about investments, this book will walk you through it all, step-by-step, leaving you feeling totally confident and ready to take retirement on.

Many retirement guides are written to help the wealthy get wealthier—focusing on tax avoidance techniques, some of which are extremely complicated and most are unnecessary for the general population.

This book was written for people who want to make the most of their retirement—retirees who have above average assets and want to make the most of their time, mind, and money during this important phase of their life. If that's you, you've come to the right place.

Here's to your success!

Sincerely,
Ken Mahoney

Mindset: The Power of Your Subconscious

While many other retirement books may start out with a chapter on why retirement is so important, and what you need to do to be prepared for yours, I'm going to start with what I consider the most basic tool of all: your mindset. Attitude, mindset and your mental state are all the first keys to your retirement success.

How many times have you heard that your attitude determines your altitude? It's true! Now let's start our ascent to 30,000 miles.

This is what I call the 'psychology' or mindset of retirement:

Your subconscious is a powerful tool that can be harnessed to help you achieve your life's goals before and during retirement, to be successful and truly happy. It's like a storeroom for everything not currently being used by your conscious mind, like your memories or your beliefs or skills you haven't used in the last few years but you know you have. For example, when learning something new, it is nearly impossible to multi-task and focus on what you're learning at the same time, but after a while, you can accomplish the task and do other things at the same time. It becomes your auto-pilot button and allows you to focus on other things after being programmed into your subconscious.

When you have a positive attitude, what you need to do becomes automatic as your conscious mind is no longer required. Your subconscious can be programmed just like a computer. But just like a computer, it has rules and 'errors' can still pop up so it's best to know what those are, so that you can program your mind effectively.

No Differential between Visualization and Reality

Your subconscious mind cannot differentiate between what is real and what is fictional. It automatically believes something to be real regardless of whether you know it's not. If you've watched a horror movie and paid attention to how you've reacted, you'd notice that you feel fear and your pulse races even though you are aware of the fact that you are not in any danger. This aspect can be used to one's advantage because through repeated visualization, the subconscious can make anything you present it with real. Let's think about what you need to do to get out of debt for a successful retirement; if you visualize success as becoming debt free, your subconscious will believe that there is no reason why you can't get out of debt, and you will find yourself looking at the task positively, with a new sense of strength and confidence.

Time Moves Faster

When you do something fun, you realize that time always moves faster than when you're doing something that you consider a job, a chore, or just something you really don't enjoy doing. When you're doing something you don't actually want to do, you form the habit of looking at your watch or the clock and time seems to stand still. This is because your subconscious recognizes that you habitually look at your watch during this particular activity and why time never seems to move. The same can be said for when you're asleep, you don't notice time passing because it's only your conscious mind that's asleep. So when you're trying to achieve your goals and you make it fun, time will pass by in a flash and the quicker you will reach them.

The Harder It Believes, The Harder It Is To Change

The more the subconscious mind believes something to be true, the harder it is to convince the subconscious that it isn't. If you have a long withstanding belief or view about something, it can be harder to change it. For example, people losing weight believe that something isn't tasty even though it's good for them. The longer they've held that belief the harder it will become to try and change it so that they will eat the healthier foods. It's very important to look ahead at your retirement and believe that you can accomplish what it takes to retire successfully; and not just for a few years, but for the duration of your retirement. The more you cement the ideas of "I can" and "I will" the more you will find that rather than dreading the thought of retirement and all that comes with it, you are actually happily anticipating the day and eager to get there as soon as possible.

Every Thought Causes a Physical Reaction

If you think that you're going to do poorly in something, then you are going to do poorly. The thought has been embedded into the subconscious and therefore the physical reaction is that you don't focus on the task or activity. However, if you think something like, 'I'm going to run and lose weight,' then when you run, you'll lose weight because your mind is turning that thought into a physical reaction. Your subconscious mind will do everything in its power to make that thought come true.

> *"Change the way you look at things and the things you look at change."* ~ *Dr. Wayne Dyer (famous quote)*

Setting goals is very important when it comes to your retirement and I'll be talking about that a little later on—it's important to have something to achieve, to see yourself in the place you want to be at in the future. Without goals, you have no reason to work hard to achieve anything and you will find yourself struggling to retire.

Everyone has goals throughout their lives, things they want to achieve in their careers, their personal lives and their retirements; you just have to look deep into yourself and find out what yours are.

Proof Strengthens Your Beliefs

If you believe yourself to be fat and someone says that you are, it just further cements into your mind that you are fat. However, if you believe that you are healthy, that you are beautiful and fit, all you have to do is find proof from those who care about you to cement that you are indeed those things.

Even you can cement them by saying out loud that you are those things and it becomes proof enough for your subconscious to be believed. It's important to believe in yourself, in your capabilities and strengths.

People who are in debt struggle to get out of it when they have a negative attitude. Staying positive on your journey towards retirement and after is crucial.

Subconscious Wins against Conscious

No matter what, your subconscious mind will win in an argument against your conscious mind. If you have a fear and even though you consciously believe you have nothing to be afraid of and you come in contact with that fear, your subconscious mind will win out. Because the subconscious mind is more powerful than the conscious one, it's important to train the subconscious to win against any unworthy conscious thoughts.

Thinking ahead about your retirement with dread or unease will make it harder for you to succeed.

New Ideas—Replacing the Old Ones

Once a new idea has been accepted by the subconscious mind, the old idea has been replaced. Say you think that lettuce is rabbit food. If you replace that idea with the fact that a salad is a great way to get vitamins and stay healthy and you accept that fact as truth, you will no longer think lettuce is rabbit food.

Avoid Conscious Effort

The more you try to obtain something with your conscious mind, the less your subconscious will respond. If you will yourself to consciously sleep, you won't sleep because it involves conscious effort. Your subconscious should be doing everything for you and the more you try to seize control with your conscious mind, the less likely it is to happen.

This may sound like 'mind games', but even Olympic athletes use visualization techniques to help them achieve their goals. I want you to have a "Gold Medal" in retirement and use this 'secret' to retirement fulfillment.

Suggestions Can Program the Subconscious

Basically, the subconscious mind will accept anything you tell it providing that the conscious mind isn't present at the time. The key behind hypnosis is that you can implant a suggestion inside a person's mind, like 'You hate smoking', and their subconscious mind will believe it providing that the conscious mind isn't present at the time the suggestion is made.

Now that you understand the rules behind this vital resource, you can manipulate it to work towards helping you achieve your goals. Just because a goal seems impossible to grasp, doesn't mean it is impossible.

A New Way To Look At Retirement

The reason why I am 'dwelling' on this concept is that we have old tapes that are on continuous play about money.

And if they were positive thoughts about money, we would continue to let the tapes play.

However, for most of us, we have negative subconscious beliefs/tapes that play:

"Money doesn't grow on trees"

"Money is the root of all evil"

"I can never have enough money"

"I may outlive my money"

"What if I go broke"

So on, and so on.

None of the above 'tapes' will help you feel good about money.

Psychology: You Have to Want it to Get It

"Make sure you have a written plan for your retirement, and review that plan on an annual basis."
~ Barry Harris, Accountant

Visualize Your Future

You're not alone if you don't have a picture of what your retirement might look like. But there are ways to visualize your future. If you cannot picture your life after retirement, then first determine whether you can picture or vocalize your life dreams or your dreams for your children or grandchildren. If you cannot do any of this, ask yourself questions such as these: How did you achieve goals over your lifetime, including your financial goals? How did they happen? Did you plan? Can you use these same tools and techniques to picture your life during retirement?

Ask yourself this question: 'If a doctor told me that my life would end in five to six years, and I would be as healthy during that period as I am now, what would I like to do or accomplish during that time so that at the end of my life I had no regrets?' Try to be as specific as possible with your answers.

Then, if you have minor children, re-answer the question but now assume that your children are grown and have had good starts in life.

Remember that the accumulation of wealth is not an end, but rather the means to accomplish your lifetime goals. You have to know your desired destinations or goals in order to develop an 'interactive road map' or 'GPS', for where you are headed, what side trips or adventures are planned along the way, and how you will experience the joys which can be found in the close relationships you have fostered with family and friends.

It's All In The Mindset

Having the right mindset to achieve anything in life is one of the most important aspects in reaching your goals because both failure and success are the results of a certain state of mind. One of the most important steps to becoming financially free and achieving everything you want before and after retirement is a change in mindset, and this must happen before anything else.

"Think and Grow Rich" by Napoleon Hill (1920) talked about this and reached two main findings:

1. All successful and wealthy people documented have certain characteristics; in fact, he was able to list all of the 17 common characteristics.
2. He also discovered that no one was born with those elements of success. So while all successful people had these 17 characteristics in common, none were born with them – they were developed over time.

An important part to achieving success is first understanding and determining what it is you want. The stronger the desire and reason to achieve something, the quicker and easier it is to achieve. You really need to take a moment to think of the reasons you want to achieve success and build wealth for your retirement before starting the journey. Your reasons provide the fuel and drive for achieving success. This could be anything as it is different for each person, but if there was one common thing that I learned from all of my clients it is that they all know what they want and why.

You must believe that you can achieve a successful retirement full of wealth and happiness before you will ever be able to accomplish it. The limits to which you subject yourself are the limits that will prevent it from happening. If you look for reasons rather than results, then you will have sabotaged yourself before you ever make it out of the starting gate. Believe that you can have it, that it can happen, and it will.

> *"A real decision is measured by the fact that you've taken a new action. If there's no action, you haven't truly decided."* ~ Anthony Robbins

Goal Setting

Very little in life can be accomplished without first setting goals. It's not likely that a person wandering aimlessly will accomplish very much. *This is your GPS for your retirement.*

Now that you're aware of the fact that you have to think about what you want in order to achieve it—that your own positive outlook on life can not only affect your life, but actually create it—you are now ready to make some changes. In order to do that, it's necessary to set some goals and give yourself a few guidelines to help yourself become better aware of what it is you want to accomplish exactly.

There's no doubt that we live in a world where there are certain laws that we are stuck or blessed with. It doesn't matter if we want to or if we acknowledge it. For example, when Newton saw the apple fall, there was no chance it was going to go up or sideways instead of down—the law of gravity in action. Additionally, in order to see that apple fall, he either had to drop it himself or wait for it to drop from the tree.

Now, in his case, it's possible he was lounging under an apple tree and the law of gravity simply 'fell in his lap'. But if he was out to accomplish something along the lines of proving the law of gravity, he would have to have had a plan to DO something. He couldn't be squashing apples in a press for cider, collecting rotten ones from beneath a tree for pig feed, or watching his wife bake a pie and hope to learn about the law of gravity.

The same applies to your situation. In order to accomplish your goals towards retirement, you have to have a plan of action in place and set goals that you can and will attain.

First of all, you have to accept that everything in your life is something that you have brought to yourself through your positive or negative mindset. When people pause to consider that, they immediately want to deny it, not wishing to take the blame for their life.

That's understandable, we are human after all and realizing that you are the source of your unhappiness or lack of success in life is hard to take in.

Who wants to believe sliding off a slippery road or falling down the stairs was something they brought to themselves? But the truth is, that's exactly what happened. Deepak Chopra says, "You and I are essentially infinite choice-makers. In every moment of our existence, we are in that field of all possibilities where we have access to an infinity of choices."

Bob Doyle, facilitator in mastering the law of attraction lets us in on the unvarnished truth stated: "Most of us attract by default. We just think that we don't have any control over it. Our thoughts and feelings are on autopilot, so everything is brought to us by default."

Now, do we want to just let everything happen to us or do we want to be in charge of the situation? Being in charge sounds a whole lot better and to do that, a plan with goals is a necessity. So, how to accomplish that?

For starters, after having examined yourself as you did in the first chapter; you now need to determine what it is you really want. Once you've done that, it becomes a process: to ask, to believe and then to receive.

To determine that, you need to first settle on what it is you want to do with your life; determine what you want and also reveal what your major concerns and worries are so that you are consciously aware of what may stand in your way.

Goals can become the incredible driving force behind the utilization of all your strengths.

People with clearly written goals accomplish far more in a shorter period of time than people without them could ever imagine. Are you convinced of the importance of goals and setting them clearly yet? Okay, here's how to go about doing it.

The journey of goal-setting is a deeply personal one. This is YOU we are talking about so your commitment has to be very personal and crystal clear. Get ready because this is going to take some initiative, time, paper and pen and self-discipline. It isn't as easy as simply kicking back; thinking about what you want and having it magically materialize in front of you. It will take some work; you're working on the ability to consciously respond to your life and create your deepest desires.

In connection with goal setting, you first have to know what it is you really desire and write it down. The more detailed the better. It can be more than one goal, just as long as there is clarity in what it (they) is (are).

And it's a good idea to have a timeframe attached to your goal, so write down what your goal is and by what date you intend to accomplish it.

The Seeker May Have To Spend Some Time Organizing

If there are several goals on your list, the next step is to prioritize them. Decide what the number one goal you wish to accomplish is. Write them down in order of importance and be sure to give them your attention; read them every day and reassert their importance in your life.

Teach yourself to observe your life even as you are living it. Looking at the world in this manner will allow you to respond to challenges and obstacles as they arise determining the next step in your journey. As you become more and more adept at this challenge, you will discover a new ease in handling all that is created in your life. You will greatly improve your ability to be clear about what you want and about the steps you have to take to bring your desires and goals to life. It takes a bit of practice to break, not only a lifetime of habits – your own – but to go counter to the programming we've all inherited through generations of wrong thinking.

So take a minute and write down the three most important goals in your life right now. Also, make note of what your three most pressing problems are right now. You're not too busy and you **do** have the time to do it—so do it now.

(or I will come find you and …)

With your goals now set, it's time to create a plan, steps you intend to take to accomplish your goals.

You've thought about what gives you the greatest feeling of accomplishment, satisfaction and value—what you really love to do. You may have considered what you would wish for if you could have anything you wanted. You've assembled your list of goals. You have to be clear about it all because if you aren't then all you have achieved is confusing yourself more, and sending out mixed signals that you won't be able to follow through with.

Now, Here's Where It Gets Good!

As a side issue, perhaps you're a bit uncertain as to what goals to put first—what you really want. It may have been a hard decision for you, maybe this is the first time in your life you have emerged from the cloud of simply living day to day to actually ask yourself what inspires you, what brings you joy and what you want. That is another aspect of putting your desires and goals down on paper. If you are uncertain and have a choice to make but don't know what to do – just keep asking yourself!

Jack Canfield, originator of the Chicken Soup for the Soul Series and founder of the Transformational Leadership Council said, "Most of us have never allowed ourselves to want what we truly want, because we can't see how it will develop."

Thus spurs the need for goals and clarity – and a plan. What will you do to keep your mind positive and seeking achievement of your goals?

Focus on the affirmative of what you're trying to accomplish. Imagine yourself in the place you want to be, everything has been accomplished, what you have asked for has manifested. What would that look like and how did you get there?

A plan is a pretty simple thing. It is basically what you are going to do to get to where you need to be. What are you willing to give to have that happen?

Now, before you go thinking, "Wait, this isn't bringing my goals and desires to life, this is work!" Well, yes, it is work. If your goal is for you to enjoy a long retirement, take a new direction and bring in more money, you need to have a course of action to bring that into being. For example, are you going to have to get out of debt, pay off your mortgage, make smart investment choices and decide how you want to spend your retirement years?

If your main goal is to retire somewhere sunny in Europe, your plan may include researching the best locations for retirees, comparing property prices, ensuring that you have enough money to get you there and the ability to maintain a satisfactory lifestyle, whatever makes you feel good to do. Conversely, don't do something that you believe could help, but you really hate. That puts you on the wrong frequency to receive what it is you're asking for.

A plan, straight forward with clear steps to follow, helps you to organize your thoughts into clarity, to focus on your goal more sharply and thus feel what it is like to be where you want to be. It's a roadmap of sorts, one that keeps you laser-focused on your goal.

A plan also puts you in the position of valuing your goals. Not simply jotting them down, reading them once or twice and tossing them aside. Always bear in mind that your current thoughts are creating your future life. Again, what you think about the most, whatever is your point of focus, is what will appear in your life.

Goals and a plan to accomplish them create a point of focus. Action enhances that focus even more. And, luckily for us all, when we take action to achieve our goals, when action is inspired because it will help us to reach our goals, it becomes effortless and feels wonderful.

Since feeling happy and grateful, and enjoying the emotion of love are powerful tools to achieving what you want out of life, then the steps you plan to take to accomplish your goal should evoke those feelings in you. Expectation is a powerful attractive force. Doing something to further your goal with the expectation that you will receive what you've asked for while eschewing any expectation of things you don't want draws it to you.

Visualization is a powerful tool to couple with expectation. The process of creating pictures in your mind of where you will be when your goal is accomplished generates energizing thoughts and feelings of having it in the present. Create those pictures with detail, following the plan you've created to reach your goal.

Here is an 'assignment': Get a bunch of your favorite magazines, poster board, scissors, and some glue. Yes, you know what comes next. I have actually have done this 'exercise' at seminars. You might think it's for 3rd graders. But I can't begin to tell you how much the participants enjoyed this part of the seminar. I happen to have my poster here as a write. There are pictures of the Caribbean, Europe and other places we enjoy traveling to. There is also a picture of a golfer, hiker, etc. It actually brings me a smile when I see it. So what are you waiting for? Get your magazines out and get busy!

To get where you're going, set those goals—set them forth with absolute clarity and confidence that they will be attained. Next, create a plan from which to proceed. Do things to further your cause that you really enjoy doing.

Retirement Goals Worksheet

Use this worksheet as a guideline for creating retirement goals and aspirations. Fill in your answers to the questions, jot down notes, and make some kind of record of your goals. Make sure to write your answers in a positive way.

A New Way To Look At Retirement

1. I want to spend my time (list at least three activities):

- 1.

- 2.

- 3.

2. A day in the life of my retirement will look like this (not to create a rigid schedule, but paint a picture of what a day in retirement life may look like in a positive way):

3. How will these activities make me feel (list at least three adjectives)?

- 1.
- 2.
- 3.

4. How will these activities help me or help others?

- 1.
- 2.
- 3.

5. Write out three positive statements that pertain to your retirement (i.e., "I have enough money coming in to live comfortably and to share with my family and favorite charities" or "I am setting a great example for my grandchildren, sharing my best experiences and what I've have learned in life.") Statements like these will help to erase some of the negative thoughts we have swirling around in our heads.

- 1.

- 2.

- 3.

Why Plan for Retirement Now?

Now, before beginning to discuss how to go about planning for your retirement, you need to understand why it's so important to take your retirement into your own hands. It might seem like a strange question, but it might surprise you to learn that many of the components that are the keys to planning for a successful retirement contradict popular beliefs about the best methods for saving for the future. To explain, let's look at the reasons behind planning for retirement.

Uncertainty in Pension Benefits and Social Security Programs

It's important to be honest about the long-term prospects of government programs to sponsor retirement. Honestly – they are not too great. Whole generations of people in the developed world are getting older, and there aren't enough working-age people filling the spaces they leave behind as they retire. As a result, fewer and fewer people are paying into Social Security.

A 2005 comprehensive study conducted by Stephen C. Goss, the Chief Actuary of the SSA (Social Security Administration) showed that the ratio of beneficiaries to covered workers under US Social Security has gone down alarmingly. In 1940, 35.3 million workers across the US paid into the Social Security system and only 222,000 beneficiaries were drawing from it. That is a ratio of 159:1. By 2003 the number of workers had increased to 154.3

million, but with a staggering and disproportionate increase in the number of beneficiaries: 46.8 million. That's a ratio of only 3.3 to 1.

Similar patterns are showing up in European pension systems and similar programs worldwide, and the burden will only grow greater. More and more people are retiring, and with modern medical advances are living decades longer than previous generations.

This effect has the potential to put a great deal of strain and drain on the system. It might leave governments with no options other than reducing or eliminating social security benefits.

Even private pension plans are at risk. Corporations sometimes fail or collapse, as can be seen with the very high-profile Enron bankruptcy at the beginning of the 2000's. This can leave any employer-sponsored stock holdings or pension plans completely worthless.

Defined benefit pension plans are meant to guarantee their participants a pre-set monthly pension for their retirement, but they are no more stable. Sometimes they fail and shut down entirely. Others try to compensate, necessitating benefit reductions or increased contributions from participants.

Additionally, employers looking to avoid the liability and increased expenses of defined benefit pension plans are switching to offering defined contribution plans instead. For many people this makes a financially stable retirement even less certain.

This has caused the widespread transfer of responsibility for financing that stable retirement. Before, this was the responsibility of the employers and the government. Now, it is the responsibility of the individual. To ensure your financial security in your golden years, it is important to take your retirement planning into your own hands and not rely on Social Security.

I do believe that Social Security will be around for quite some time. To maintain Social Security it is my belief that taxes will increase and benefits will begin at a later age.

The situation isn't completely dire – the social security system is not completely guaranteed to fail. But even if it stays operating for decades to come, betting your whole retirement on money that isn't yours yet might be risky. Not to mention that Social Security is not meant to provide a luxurious standard of living. It is only meant to serve as a minimum safety net, guaranteeing a minimum of comfort for your twilight years.

Sudden, Unexpected Medical Expenses

If you don't have your own reserve of funds to draw on, you will have a difficult time acquiring very much past that minimum standard of living that Social Security guarantees. And if your health were to fail, your financial situation could quickly spiral out of control.

Unless you're very lucky, aging will bring new ailments with it, and all of them come with new healthcare expenses. If you don't have any money set aside, it can prove difficult trying to balance those expenses with maintaining your standard of living, especially if you or a loved one becomes ill. To avoid having your retirement savings destroyed by unexpected health issues, you can look into insurance options for medical care as well as long-term care insurance.

"There are generally three things that can jeopardize financial security in our later years: reckless or ill-advised investments, suffering a major medical problem without adequate insurance coverage, and paying for long-term care—the kind of care not covered by medical insurance plans—for a protracted period of time. The potential to incur long-term care expenses is significant in the face of advances in medical care and with so many people living more healthy lifestyles. To address this potential risk to financial security everyone should develop a long term care plan, investigating all of their real available resources, including the possibility of purchasing long-term care insurance."

~ Les Von Losberg, CLU, cHFC

Keeping Your Options Open

Life can be very unpredictable. Unforeseen illnesses, sudden expenses, and the rising uncertainty of pension systems are only a few of thousands of potential sources of financial strain. No matter which of life's many challenges you end up facing, having some funds set aside will help you pass through them, by giving you the flexibility to take care of problems comfortably and immediately when they arise, so that the unexpected doesn't immediately turn your life upside down. A substantial savings 'nest egg' can give you some serious peace of mind.

Estate Planning

Of course, saving for the future doesn't have to be about preparing for calamities. There are lighter, softer reasons for bolstering your retirement savings. Your savings could help you contribute to the lives of your children or grandchildren in a multitude of ways – financing current or future education, passing on your savings, or making sure a family member will own your assets with sentimental value, like heirlooms, or even land and real estate.

Without a concrete and secure 'nest egg' on which to base your retirement, you may end up forced to sell off assets to cover the expenses of your twilight years. This can leave you with no money to leave your children, or even make you a financial burden to your loved ones.

Dealing With Your Retirement Worries

When it comes to retirement, there's plenty to worry and dream about. But according to a recent survey, the three biggest worries that clients of financial advisers face seem somewhat easy to solve.

In a survey we conducted, we found that slightly more than eight in 10 advisers say their clients' top dream is greater financial security in retirement.

According to the advisers surveyed, their clients' greatest retirement worries are, in order, outliving their savings (87%); enjoying their current quality of life in retirement (79%); and affording good medical care (70%).

Not surprisingly, the survey showed that clients who can "easily visualize their financial dreams may be less worried about retirement." But the survey also showed that not everyone is spending much time visualizing. Only one in 10 advisers said their clients find it "easy to picture their financial dreams."

This is why I use a holistic approach with my clients. It goes well beyond numbers. The process incorporates many of the items already discussed in this book.

Given these worries, we posed two questions to those in the business of giving advice: one, what would you tell Americans to do to alleviate their greatest worries? And two, what would you say to Americans who can't picture their financial dreams?

Dealing With Your Worries

In general, when it comes to dealing with your worries, it's important to separate the ones that have some merit from the ones that don't. After distinguishing between the two, you can then do some 'what ifs' and develop a planning or coping response for each worry.

In psychology, this technique is called stress inoculation training. This technique, also used in training pilots in simulators where they learn how to fly under both ideal and nightmare conditions so that, if the nightmare actually happens, the pilot is better able to respond rationally. The same holds true for those planning for retirement. (And fortunately we don't have to simulate this with you flying a plane!)

It's easy to understand why Americans are worried right now, given what happened in 2008. Events such as this in financial history cause people to suffer from the behavioral finance concept known as anchoring. Under the anchoring process, people latch onto a belief that may or may not be true and apply it as a reference point for future decisions.

The best way to deal with anchoring is to acknowledge that it exists and try to avoid the negative emotions associated with the particular historical event.

Besides using stress inoculation training and acknowledging anchoring bias, advisers say there are least three steps to take to overcome your worries.

First and foremost, put in place a comprehensive financial plan.

Far too many individuals miss out on substantial opportunities to save on interest payments, taxes, and expenditures, and make poor financial decisions because they have never had an experienced financial planner sit down and discuss all aspects of their planning with them. Additionally, many Americans lack self-control when it comes to their finances; a good financial planner can utilize various tools and methods to assist clients with the necessary self-control to save enough and make smart financial decisions.

Secondly, ignore short-term market movements, unless you have designs on re-balancing your investment portfolio. Adopt a strategic asset allocation for the long term, and stick with it.

And lastly, remember that because of their inherent volatility, stocks and stock mutual funds are long-term investments. In order to achieve the higher long-term returns that the stock market offers, you'll need to diversify, diversify, diversify; keep total fees and costs associated with investments reasonably low; invest tax-efficiently; and adhere to the long-term plan you adopt for your future.

The Seven Keys
To a Successful Retirement Plan

You can't calculate your 'number' unless you have a clear vision of what you want your retirement to be.

Your plan has to begin with a reasonable consideration of how you want to live your life, what kinds of things will be important to you, and where you want to spend your time. If you can create a lifestyle plan first, the financial plan is far easier and more realistic to design.

The 'number' doesn't mean much if it isn't tied directly to your retirement lifestyle plan.

Once you have clarified the vision, we can work together to develop a realistic financial plan to make it happen.

While there are many ways to structure a retirement plan, here is a suggestion that has worked well for investors. If you think of your retirement plan using this framework, it will not only help you develop a long-term strategy, but also make your transition into this next phase of life far clearer for you.

Key One: Visualize Your Ideal Retirement Lifestyle

As you look forward to retired life, what kinds of things will be important to you? Many of the boomers that I meet with think of retirement as a series of leisure activities strung together over a long period of time—it is almost like they are planning for a thirty-year long weekend!

While your future will no doubt be full of exciting and meaningful activities, the fact is that you are still "living your life". What does an average week look like for you? What kinds of things will you value in this next phase of life, and what would you consider to be 'fulfilling' activities for you?

Also, what things might change over time as you move through the various stages of your retirement?

You don't need to write a fifty-page retirement planning manual to prepare for the future, but you should look at retirement as a lifestyle transition rather than a 'new' life. If your retirement means that you now have more freedom, a reasonable question to ask yourself is how you can use that freedom to live the kind of life you really want.

My suggestion is that you think about the first five years of your retirement life first and then create some longer-term vision beyond that. Don't forget that things may change over time as a result of changes in health, circumstance or your own attitudes. The vision has to be fluid and flexible!

Once you have developed your blueprint for the first five years, you can then turn your attention to the major areas of your retirement life.

Key Two: Take a Close Look at Your Health and Your Plans for Healthy Aging

While this may seem obvious, a lot of people think of physical health without paying much attention to mental health. In retirement, it will likely be your mental health that influences your physical well-being.

Retirement is all about attitude. (Remember earlier when we spoke about your attitude determines your altitude? I hope you get a lot of frequent flyer miles in retirement planning!)

Successful retirees believe they can control certain elements of their life, are committed to living each and every day to the fullest, and continue to challenge themselves to do new things, go new places and practice life-long learning.

The more optimistic and positive you are mentally in retirement, the more likely you will be to pay attention to your physical health. After all, if retirement life is going to be this good, you might as well try to stay around for a long time!

Key Three: Take a Positive Attitude Towards 'Work'

For many retirees, work is a welcome break from leisure. It is one of those positive stresses that can energize you and keep you connected to your community. Work can also give your life meaning and remind you that you are still active and involved.

Work doesn't even have to be for pay. Many turn to volunteering as a way to give back or to "self-actualize".

The bottom line is that you want to use work as a positive contributor to your retirement life, using your time, energy and experience to benefit your community and yourself. Remember that old adage: "If you love what you do, you never have to work again!"

Key Four: Create and Nurture Meaningful Relationships

In this next phase of life, much of your happiness will come from the quality of the personal relationships you enjoy. This will include your family, your close personal friends and your social network.

Consider the relationships that will be important to you, and make sure that you continue to nurture and support them. You will also want to find ways to add to your social network so that people who can add to the quality of your retirement life surround you.

Key Five: Take a Balanced Approach to Leisure

Most retirement plans are really 'leisure' plans. One of the most exciting things about retirement is that you can do the kind of things that really give you pleasure and life enjoyment.

Successful retirees recognize that the more balance they have in their leisure activities, the more they will enjoy each thing they do. For example, golf or travel every day may sound like an ideal way to spend your time, but will too much golf or travel actually take away from your enjoyment of each activity?

Key Six: Make Sure That Your Home Always Meets Your Needs

You want your retirement home to be a source of comfort to you, not stress. There may come a time when you don't want to shovel snow or spend time cleaning a big home. Remember also that a three-floor condo with lots of stairs may sound okay today, but could prove to be impractical somewhere down the line.

Once you have considered these six keys to your retirement strategy, you can focus on:

Key Seven: Use Your Financial Resources to Make Your Retirement Plans Happen

I call this financial comfort, and it is the goal of any good financial plan for retirement.

Getting Out of Debt

Debt Is a Sum Owed; A State Of Owing; An Obligation

Debt is that which is owed; usually referencing assets owed, but the term can also cover moral obligations and other interactions not requiring money. In the case of assets, debt is a means of using future purchasing power in the present before a summation has been earned. Some companies and corporations use debt as a part of their overall corporate financial strategy.

A debt is created when a creditor agrees to lend a sum of assets to a debtor. In modern society, debt is usually granted with expected repayment; in most cases, plus interest.

Personal Debt

While in some business situations, debt is actually a way towards creating growth; the inverse is true when it comes to personal debt or consumer debt. Of course over the past couple of years, we have seen how banks have used derivatives and loans on risky ventures to bring economies to the brink of disaster. Bank bailouts or situations such as Greece, where projected defaults on loans led to billions being loaned to cover the country so its debt wouldn't destroy it, prove that even savvy finance leaders don't always have the skinny on how too much debt can affect even a huge institution or a country.

Nevertheless, we aren't a country, but individuals who don't have the luxury of the International Monetary Fund to bail us out of debt. So we need to determine what that type of debt ours is, and how we can eliminate it with our rapid debt reduction system.

Consumer debt is debt which is used to fund consumption rather than investment and remains unpaid. e.g. goods or service purchases made using a credit card and that credit card has not been cleared or fully paid off since the original purchase. This is not 'good debt', as interest rates are high and there is not a tax write off.

Those who are highly in debt have not found the way to 'money maturity'. There are different stages I believe to 'money maturity'. The stage of high debt is living in a false lifestyle. One can live 'abundantly', without going into debt.

Assessment: One's personal financial situation can be assessed by compiling simplified versions of financial balance sheets and income statements.

Balance Sheet: A personal balance sheet lists the values of personal assets (e.g., car, house, clothes, stocks, bank account), along with personal liabilities (e.g., credit card debt, bank loan, mortgage).

Income Statement: A personal income statement lists personal income and expenses.

Personal net worth is the difference between an individual's total assets and total liabilities. Our goal in this guide is to help you reduce your debt (liabilities) and decrease the difference between your assets and liabilities and thereby increase your net worth.

Some interesting statistics to show that you are not alone if you have debt:

- Of those people who have credit cards, about 10% have total card balances greater than $10,000.
- 36% of those people have an annual total household income under $50,000 and 13% have household incomes under $30,000.
- About 1 in 8 people use 80% or more of their credit card limit.
- Bankruptcy cases filed in U.S. Federal courts totaled 1,042,993 for the 12-month period ending September 30, 2008. On average, using national averages, 3.38 people out of every 1000 people, filed for either Chapter 7 Bankruptcy or Chapter 13 Bankruptcy.

What Do I Do NOW To Bring Down My Debt

"Many credit reports contain reporting errors that unjustly lower credit scores. Since credit scores can largely determine loan approval, interest rate, and monthly payments; it's important to review your credit reports before applying for financing (giving yourself time to make corrections). Making sure your credit scores are as high as possible is smart money management!"

~ Helayne Urban
Helayne Urban Credit Coach, Inc.

Pre-Retirement

By reducing or eliminating debt, you can help save for when you're older and ready to tell the world where it can go. Budgeting is a proven way to help manage, reduce, and eventually eliminate debt. Start by drafting a list of your monthly income for both yourself and your spouse (if married).

This is Kat and her husband, John's income:

Total Income:	$7831.18
Gross(Kat's) $5,833	70,000 ÷ 12 = 5,833
Gross (John's) $3,750	45,000 ÷ 12 = 3,750
Net (Kat's) $4,569	5,833 x 21.68% (effective tax rate) = 1,264 5,833 – 1,264 = 4,569
Net (John's) $2,937	3,750 x 21.68% = 813 3,750 – 813 = 2,937
Other income $125.18	Small Business income
Other Income $200.00	Independent Cosmetic Sales $200.00

Now that you know what it is you make in a month on a net basis (after taxes), you need to list both your Fixed and your Variable expenses. Fixed expenses would be the mortgage or the car loan while a Variable expense would be the non-fat mocha latte at Starbucks – or three – that you have each day.

Kat and John's fixed expenses don't surpass their total monthly income.

Fixed Expenses	Total Fixed Expenses: $1280.00
Mortgage	$500.00
Electric	$150.00
Oil & Water Heating	$150.00
House Insurance	$120.00
Car Payment	$150.00
Car Insurance	$150.00
Cable/Satellite	$80.00
Telephone	$40.00
Cell Phone	$100.00
Internet	$120.00
Health Insurance	$50.00
Life Insurance	$50.00

However, their variable expenses (seen on the next page) are leaving them with little left to save for retirement.

Variable Expenses	Total Variable Expenses: $5830.00	
Allowances	$1000.00	
Car Fuel	$600.00	
Car Maintenance	$80.00	
Public Transit	$0.00	
Tolls/Taxi's/Parking	$2,400	
Medical/Dental	$200.00	
Groceries/Clothes	$400.00	
Pets	$75.00	
Family/Gifts	$150.00	
Vacation	$0.00	
Charities	$100.00	
Restaurants	$75.00	
Entertainment	$100.00	
Hobbies/Sports	$50.00	
Clubs/Unions	$150.00	
Bank Fees*	$50.00	
Emergency Fund*	$100.00	
Savings*	$250.00	
Debt Repayments*	$500.00	
Total Expenses: $7,681.00*	Total Income: $7,831.18*	Left Over: $150.18*

Looking over Kat and John's budget sheet, anything with an asterisk is an uncontrollable number. You can't change them no matter how long you try and Jedi Mind Trick the people in charge. However, the other colors, especially the numbers in orange, can be changed. There is no reason why those numbers cannot decrease and the savings put towards your retirement portfolio.

Find a compromise with your budget. Instead of buying that Latte every day, have one on Friday to celebrate the end of the work week. Instead of going to the movies every weekend, have a movie night at home with a film rented from the public library – it's free!

It's amazing how you can live 'abundantly', without spending a lot of money.

Now, before you go dumping the money you've just saved into your portfolio – stop. Remember the very end of the list with that lovely heading of DEBT? Start repaying your debts *first* before trying to save money for later. I'm not saying not to put anything away, but just to do so in moderation until your debts are erased.

After Retirement

If you are retired but are struggling to stay that way, all is not lost. Like with those who are planning for their retirement, making and adhering to a budget AFTER can help you stay retired comfortably.

Unlike the Pre-Retirement budget sheet, there are now options to consider when looking things over. If you're paying a mortgage on a large house but do not intend to spend as much time living in it or there's no longer a need to own something so large, then it may be time to consider moving.

Yes, moving does cost money but depending on the value of the property you are sitting on and what you require for a new home, it may not be as costly to do; especially if you arrange to move your pre-existing mortgage right along with you.

Your Personal Retirement Roadmap

If you've purchased this book, you've probably been long dreaming about how great retirement is going to be. Think about it … having the freedom to play golf, having a long leisurely lunch with friends, visiting your children and grandchildren, traveling or doing some volunteering. But, do you know what may be a surprise to you? I actually have many clients who tell me they never wanted to retire! They really like what they do, and the thought of not working is foreign to them! It's true!

You may not want to retire, but you should still make plans so you are able to stop working if you choose (or are forced to). Age creeps up on everyone. You might feel fine right now, your spouse may be healthy and you have no plans to slow down. But our bodies do age, and at some point you may not be able to work at the pace you do now. Wouldn't it be nice to have the financial resources available so you could walk away from your job on a minute's notice and never have to worry about money?

There are a number of clients I meet with who were 'forced' to retire. They were 'downsized' years earlier than they planned.

"But…but…but…" I hear you saying. "Retirement planning sounds really difficult and I'm so busy right now." Well, I've got some good news for you – retirement road-mapping doesn't have to be hard. In fact, it all boils down to just *four* questions you need to ask yourself.

The 4 questions you must ask yourself:

1. What do you want your retirement to look like? Will it be a sunny stucco home in Arizona or maybe a golfing community in Southern Florida? Or do you want to stay where you are? It's essential to decide on where you will want to live, since the cost of living varies greatly.

2. How much time do you have left before you want to retire? Now, notice I didn't say "before you retire". I said "before you WANT to retire" because increasing numbers of people are opting to retire earlier or later than 65. Sixty five isn't automatic anymore, unless you work for a company that mandates it. But in any case, you need to figure out how many years you have left before you want to retire. Time is very important in investing; it's one thing to have three hours to drive 30 miles, but if you have to go 900 miles in those three hours, a car won't cut it – you need a plane. (yet another reference to altitude!)

3. How are you doing right now on retirement planning and saving? You're going to need to be very honest about this one, because it's your starting point for the road map that's going to follow. Do you have a 401k with your employer, or does your spouse have one? Do you have a Roth IRA or a paid-off home, or do you own investment property?

4. What are your options for getting to retire on time? Some vehicles are better than others for retirement planning. For

instance, a slow, steady plan that's easy on your budget is great...if you started it at age 21 and kept at it. On the other hand, if you're starting at 50, you will need a far more aggressive strategy. When you start retirement planning, you need to look at options that have a chance of getting you there on time. There's no point in having a walking plan if your goal is to cover 600 miles in two hours, right? You need a plane.

Protecting Your Assets with Cash Equivalents

So let's talk about how to set up your own personal retirement roadmap: because without a map, you won't get there. So let's talk about investment vehicles you can use to reach your retirement goals.

Remember, you can have multiple goals that incorporate short-term, intermediate, and long term investment vehicles. It is important that you realize that you will have multiple strategies, and investments for each one.

Cash
- Certificates of Deposit (CDs)
- Money market accounts
- Money you have in savings
- Mutual funds held in money market accounts

Did you know that when you put cash in the bank or credit union you're actually making them a loan? It's true. They use your cash to lend to businesses and government agencies that want to borrow some money.

I am always asked how much cash one should have. The short answer is: it depends. It depends if you have a lot fixed versus variable expenses. It depends if you have a salary (steady) income, or a commission and variable income.

The minimum one should have in cash is 6 months of expenses.

So if cash equivalents don't pay much interest, why are they so attractive, besides the fact they're very safe investments? Well, for one thing, people who like to save money can get to it easily if they need to.

However, with this low interest rate environment, some people may have too much in short term. In the 'good ole days' when money markets were paying 5-7%, it was 'ok' to have 'too much' short term. If for example you had $200,000 in a money market earning 7%, you made $14,000 in interest.

Some banks are paying .1 to .3 % (yes, move the decimal over). Some banks require you to bring them a toaster!

At .3%, the above example of $200,000 would bring in $600 and that interest would be taxable!

However, there is still a risk; that big, bogeyman known as inflation. If inflation happens faster than the rate you're earning from your cash equivalents, then your money loses buying power. For instance, if your savings pays you 1% per year and inflation comes in that year at 3%, you aren't keeping up – you're falling behind because your purchasing power is going down.

Look at it this way - if you have $20,000 in savings and they pay you 2%, at the end of the year you'll have $20,400. But what if you want to buy a new car that cost $20,000 last year?   That same care with inflation is now priced at $20,600?   See how your money lost some purchasing traction there?

What's the solution? It is two things: the first is to look for accounts that pay you the highest possible interest rate. The second is to put away money for your intermediate and long-term goals.

FREE MONEY: Why 401k's And SEP-IRA's Are The 'New Normal'

The best thing about them is that your employer will usually match the money you put into your 401k up to a limit. However, you'll probably have to work there for a while before you get fully "vested", which means that you get the full company matching. Some companies make you wait seven years or so to become 100% vested, and have a schedule prior to that. For example, you might be 20% vested after three years, and so on until you hit seven years.

If you work for a company that offers a 401k plan, this is an excellent retirement vehicle because they may match your contributions up to a specific limit. And even if you change companies, most 401ks are portable and you can roll them over to the next company or into an IRA. Be warned though that if you take early distributions or cash out your 401k prior to age 59 1/2, you'll owe a 10% penalty PLUS taxes on what you take out!

If your company does not match, it is still advisable to put money away through the 401k.

The money that you put in your 401k will directly lead to a lower tax bill since this is pre-tax money that is going into the plan.

What about Traditional IRA's?

Traditional IRA's can work as well, because contributions to these accounts are tax-deductible (caution: the deduction is limited if you or your spouse participate in another retirement plan). Though with 401k accounts, you are allowed to put in more money pre-tax.

But it is a double-edged sword. Since you got a break when you invested, when you withdraw from it, you will have to pay tax on all the money you withdraw from the account.

Something else you must know is that there is a 10% penalty on the entire distribution if you withdraw it before aged 59-1/2, although there are some exceptions. You'll still have to pay the tax, though. The allowable exceptions to the 10% penalty on early withdrawals are:

- Any medical expenses that you were not reimbursed for and that add up to more than 7.5% of your Adjusted Gross Income (as defined by the IRS).
- If you're on unemployment and your distributions don't exceed the cost of your medical insurance.
- If you're disabled.
- If you're a spouse beneficiary of an IRA owner who passed away.
- If you took an annuity as your distribution.
- If you had qualified higher education expenses and your distribution did not exceed them.
- If you take out $10,000 that you used to buy, build or rebuild your first home.
- If you're an active duty military reservist and you've been called for more than 180 days.
- If the IRS puts a levy on you, and you need to take distributions to help cover it.

To Roth or Not To Roth?

'Always ask your CPA or accountant whether you can contribute to a Roth IRA. If you exceed the income limits, you may not be able to contribute."

~ Guy Sperduto, CPA

Roth IRA's – you don't get a tax deduction when you contribute to your Roth IRA since contributions are made with after-tax dollars.

It's tough for me to make the call for you, since a lot of the decisions of whether to invest in a Roth IRA depend on your personal situation and your own retirement roadmap, but I can tell you that Roth IRA's benefit many people.

I usually defer the 'vehicle' that you use to a CPA, or accountant. As he or she will know your income and what is most appropriate each tax year.

There are two more items about those Roth IRA's. First off, you don't have rules about when you must start taking distributions and how much. You don't have to start drawing on your Roth IRA at age 701/2, unlike other plans. This is great, because your earnings can keep on growing tax-free.

The other benefit of the Roth IRA is you can withdraw the money you contributed tax-free. So, if you do have an emergency and need the money before you retire, you can get some out tax-free. If you take out any of the earnings before age 59-1/2, there will be taxes to be paid, plus a 10% penalty. So, keep good records of the amount you contribute each year.

Dividend Paying Stocks

Stocks are called "equities" since each share represents partial ownership of a company. Companies sell shares of ownership to raise money. If you're a bit older – say, over

50 – you're probably more interested in investing in stocks that pay dividends or bonds for steady income rather than for growth … unless you're seriously behind on your investing and you feel you can take risks.

You can earn steady income in two ways from stocks:

The first is through dividends, which present the distributions of the company's profits. After all, who else would be entitled to the profits but the owners of the company – and that's you if you own stock. Generally, it's the large companies that pay dividends, and they pay them four times a year. You can usually choose whether to take your dividends in the form of a cash payment or reinvest them in buying even more shares of the company. If you're in it for retirement income, reinvest until you retire…then start taking dividends in cash.

The second way is by appreciation. This is the way you hear about most – all those stories about people making a killing in the stock markets. Large companies are generally safer investments, but smaller companies have more potential for their price to go up.

Think about it: if Big Oil Co. just made a billion dollars in profits last year, it's going to be extremely hard to double or triple that, but if Little Company Inc. made $250,000 last year, they could easily double, triple or even quadruple their earnings…or better. Be advised, though, that with stocks you could lose everything if the company goes under – so don't invest money you're not prepared to lose.

Earning Steady Income with Bonds

Bonds can be your friend if you're looking for steady income and you don't want to take chances with what inflation might do to cash equivalents...and if you're older and your priority is having your investments safe and secure. In essence, you're loaning money to someone – it's usually either a company or most often the government (Federal government or state municipality).

When you buy a bond, you get paid interest at a fixed rate for a certain period of time – that's why it's fixed income.

These are questions to ask about bonds:

1. What is the rate?
2. When are you supposed to be paid?
3. How long is the bond maturity?
4. How reliable is the borrower – AAA, AA, A, B or worse? (AAA is the best and it goes down from there.)
5. How much does the bond cost?

How much can you earn? It depends on the bond's face value, coupon rate and yield. That bond's face value is the value of the bond at maturity, which is when they pay off the loan you've made them. The most common face value is $1,000 per bond.

One thing I want to stress is that the actual market price of a bond could be more or less than the bond's face value. A bond's market price can move up and down. However, when it matures, you will get your principle value.

You'll see something on the bond called "coupon rate". A coupon rate refers to the interest that will be paid and it depends on that bond's face value. For example, if you've got a bond with a value of $1,000 and 6% coupon, then that bond will pay you a $60 a year interest.

It depends on the bond type as to how many times a year you will get paid. For bond funds, they generally pay monthly. For treasury, corporate and municipals bonds, usually twice a year.

So what happens if you buy a bond at face value? Well, your coupon rate and actual earned yield will be the same. But it doesn't always happen that way. Sometimes bonds are sold at higher or lower prices than their face values. When that happens, your actual yield can be different from the bond's coupon rate.

Here's the bottom line for you: buying a bond at a discount, or less than its face value, means you get a higher yield than the stated coupon rate. However, buying a bond at more than face value means you get a lower yield than the stated coupon rate.

So are bonds taxable or tax-free?

It all depends on where you live, the type of bond and the interest you receive from a bond investment. Generally speaking, all corporate bonds are taxable. Municipal and state bonds are usually tax exempt if you're in the same state that the issuer is located. Federal government bonds are federally taxable but watch out for a possible tax bite at the state and local levels.

Do Interest Rates Affect Prices?

Absolutely – they're inversely proportional to each other. In other words, interest rates and bonds work like a see-saw; when rates rise, bond prices go down, and when rates fall, bond prices go up.

If interest rates rise, newly issued bonds are going to pay you more than the bonds you own. This means that your older bonds will be worth less, and you would have to sell them at a discount.

But if the interest rates drop, newly issued bonds will pay lower interest than the bonds you own. Then your older bonds will typically be worth more. If you hold a bond to maturity, it doesn't matter, since price fluctuations won't affect you.

Here's another thing you need to know – an issuer can decide to pay off a bond early because of interest rates (i.e. they don't want to keep on paying that much interest). You know how you can pay off a mortgage at any time without a penalty?

Well, many bond issuers have the ability to "call" in the bonds early. Count on this ... if interest rates drop significantly, they're going to call in that bond. Why? They don't want to pay you much more than the going interest rate. This allows the bond issuer to get rid of this high interest debt and borrow again at a lower interest rate.

Can you stand to have your money tied up that long?

Before you buy a bond, you need to consider not only the risk factors (as expressed in the Moody's and Standard and Poor's ratings) but also how much interest will be paid. In general, the longer the bond period, the higher the risk that something might go wrong and therefore the higher the interest rate you can expect to earn.

As far as time goes, you've got three categories of bonds:

- Short-term bonds (generally under 2 years).
- Intermediate-term bonds (generally 2-10 years)
- Long-term bonds (generally more than 10 years).

So, consider carefully whether there's any chance at all you'll need that money in the next 2 to 10 years…and if there is, then bonds are not going to be your best choice.

How can you keep the risk down so you can sleep nights?

Financial professionals like me understand that a lot of people aren't very risk-tolerant. For that reason, we recommend holding a variety of bonds with different maturity dates.

It's the same situation you see with stocks or most types of securities – don't put all your eggs in one basket. This means to avoid holding a large bond position with a single issuer or type of bond. Bond mutual funds can also reduce risk because they invest in a pool of many bonds.

What about Good, Old-Fashioned Savings Bonds?

Back in the 1950s and '60s it was in style to buy a savings bond for a baby in his or her name and stick it away somewhere … so it might not be a bad idea to ask your parents if they have those in a safe deposit box somewhere.

These types of bonds are government bonds made just for individual investors. Because of that, there's a big limitation – they can generally only be redeemed by their original owner, except in a few circumstances. Savings bonds include:

- I bonds: if you want protection against inflation, these are the bonds you want. They pay a fixed rate, combined with a variable interest rate that's updated twice a year based on the current inflation rate.

- EE bonds: If you buy one of these that's been issued on or after May 1, 2005, you're get a fixed rate of interest. One good feature is that they increase in value every month instead of every six months…plus they compound your interest semi-annually.

The good news is that interest earned on Series EE bonds is except from state and local income taxes. You can defer federal income tax until you redeem the bonds, which will stop earning interest after 30 years.

- HH bonds: Like late-year EE bonds, HH bonds also earn a fixed rate of interest. Unlike EE bonds, HH bonds pay interest every six months until maturity or redemption; whichever comes first. Unfortunately, the US Treasury discontinued the HH series of bonds in 2004, but they will continue to honor outstanding HH bonds still held by investors…so your only option for getting them now is to buy them from other investors or brokers.

What Should You Do Right Now?

My advice is to educate yourself about retirement and investing options. Reading this chapter has already helped with that! Honestly, no one is going to care more about your money than you!

I advise people to seek out a qualified professional to help them plan their retirement. Remember, this is a long-term relationship with a trusted advisor. You need an advisor who will be with you for a long time and will guide you through the years. Things change in your life; your job, kids, marriage, college and inheritances all affect your retirement plans. Tax laws and retirement options change as well. Something that made perfect sense 10 years ago may no longer be appropriate for you, so have someone that will be there through thick and thin!

Markets and investment options change as well. Unless you want to spend the time to stay up to date on all of these changes, you should look for an experienced, trusted guide to help you.

I always use the analogy of a 'good' caddy in golf. A 'good' caddy should keep you out of sand and water (unless you golf like me). The same is true for a 'good' advisor. They should keep you out of the sand and water hazards and direct you to the green!

Investment Success (Part 1)

If you construct a building with a strong foundation based on an organized plan of assembly, your building won't just last; it will be sturdy and reliable. Just as a strong foundation is critical to the longevity of a building, a strong foundation in the logic behind your retirement investment strategy is also of great importance. Investors who don't know why they are doing what they are doing won't do it for very long—and it definitely won't be done well. The lack of discipline and an absence of proper planning are the biggest causes of failure amongst investors, especially retirees. The best way to get people to stay the course is to make sure you know the why behind your portfolio design.

In this chapter, we'll look at various asset classes and begin to discuss why proper asset allocation into a mix of these classes is essential for building a strong investment foundation for retirees who are interested in investing before and during retirement.

Evidence of the Problem

Experts conducted a number of studies to discover why people do so poorly when it comes to investments, even though the stock market delivered stellar returns throughout its history. One study has been examining investors' decisions to buy, hold, and sell mutual funds since 1984, and they found that investor behavior is the biggest deterrent to their success. Even though the market delivered returns in excess of thirteen percent from 1985 to 2004, according to their research, the average investor earned only 3.7 percent in the stock market.

What are these investors doing wrong? The biggest problem stems from not having any confidence in their investment strategies. The average investor has little patience when investing in the stock market. According to the study, investors only hold on to mutual funds for an average of approximately 2.9 years. Several other studies verify this behavioral shortcoming as well.

As I have stated on a number of the radio shows that I'm on, 'real' investors buy high and sell low. Didn't you hear we should do just the opposite?

Trim Tabs is a company that tracks inflow and outflows of the mutual fund market. In the Lehman Brothers 'crash', billions were pouring out of Stock Mutual funds on a daily basis! In fact, in 2009, tens of billions per month were coming out of stock mutual funds when the Dow Jones Industrial Average was hovering around 7000. By 2012, the Dow nearly doubled from the point.

Trim Tabs also followed the 'tech crash' of 2000. In 1999, investors were putting tens of billions into stock funds while the market was souring. The 'tech heavy' NASDAQ was over 5000. A couple years later, the NASDAQ lost nearly half its value, and guess what? You guessed it; investors were again selling in droves.

So that is why I state that most investors buy high and sell low.

The Big Secret Revealed

What if you could find out what really drives the returns you are likely to experience as an investor? Your chances of being successful would skyrocket! Isn't that every retiree's dream? Well, I have good news; such information does exist. In 1986, three academics named Gary P. Brinson, L. Randolph Hood, and Gilbert L. Beebower published a study of ninety-one pension plans and the factors that determined their performance over a ten-year period from 1974 to 1983. The authors of the study replaced the pension funds' stock, bond, and cash selections with simple indexes; and by doing so, they achieved performance that was as good as—if not better than—the professional pension managers. They repeated the study in 1991 with similar results.

The studies found that three factors were primarily responsible for the performance they witnessed in the world of pensions: 1) stock selection 2) market timing and 3) asset allocation. This study is highly useful because it gives us a glimpse into the investment strategies of some of the highest paid, best and brightest, informed investors out there— pension fund managers—who are naturally regulated by the fact that they have a fiduciary responsibility to the corporations whose pensions they manage.

The Big Picture

While all three factors play a role in portfolio performance, the vast majority of performance is driven by only one factor—the asset mix. The percentage of the performance pie that is affected by asset allocation towers over the other two variables.

Firstly, attempts at timing the market and selecting the best stocks drive investment performance down more often than not. Asset allocation is the most important aspect to focus on as an investor. Since that is the most crucial factor, let's spend some time looking at asset classes and how to define them.

Asset Classes

To use an admittedly corny example, let's say that asset classes are like a big race to which everyone is invited. Imagine seeing a full-page ad in your local newspaper announcing a huge cross-country race next week. You are invited to attend and bring the vehicle of your choice, but there's only one stipulation. You won't be told what the race course will look like. In fact, you won't know anything at all until the race starts.

On race day, the starting line is full of different types of vehicles. One person brought a snowmobile, another showed up with a motorcycle, another rode in on a dune buggy, and yet another is driving a race car. At the starting line there is a huge veil that makes it impossible to see the race course. As the starting gun fires, the veil lifts and the course is revealed. The road is snow-covered for the first patch of the race; so it is clear that the person who brought the snowmobile has the advantage in the first leg of the race. However, this doesn't mean that his advantage will last for long. The next patch of terrain may be sand. In that case, the dune buggy holds the advantage.

This is much like the world of asset class investing. We only have a clouded view of what economic terrain lies ahead. In the late 1980's, the terrain was best for international companies. In the early 1990's, the conditions were ripe for small U.S. companies. In the late 1990's, all lights were green for U.S. large stocks. The early 2000's have been great for value stocks and emerging markets. Bonds from 2007 to 2012 produced great results as interest rates sank. The bottom line is that we don't know what the future has in store, but we do know this—it will be unpredictable.

The best that investors can do is trim stocks as they rise, and allocate back into them when the market sells off.

It is like being a 'contrarian' on purpose. When everyone is excited like they were in 1999, you take some profits. As an investor, when the 'herd' was selling stocks in 2008-2009, you average in. This way you will be apt to buy low, and sell high.

Broad Diversification

As you have seen, the "vehicles" in the previous example stand for different asset classes in the investing process. These asset classes have unique characteristics that cause them to behave differently depending on what is going on in the economy. It is important to have exposure to many of these investment areas rather than betting everything on one or two of them. Narrowly investing your money in a few select areas is like betting everything on the motorcycle in the preceding example. It probably would have wiped out early in the race on the snow-covered ground. That is why it's much safer to place your bets across all of the vehicles.

Asset Class Examples

The six different asset classes we will cover in the next few sections are:

1. Treasury Bills
2. Treasury Bonds
3. Large U.S. Stocks
4. Large International Stocks
5. Small U.S. Stocks
6. Small International Stocks

Treasury Bills:

The first category is Treasury bills. When the government borrows money for less than one year they issue Treasury bills (also known as T-bills). T-bills are the standard for low-risk investing in the industry. The reason is that they mature in less than one year, so there is little interest rate risk. There is also minimal risk of default, because the government always has the option to increase taxes or print money to repay its bills.

Because there is little risk of losing money in T-bills, there is also little "risk" that you will make much money. In fact, over the past eighty years, T-bills only returned approximately 0.70 percent after inflation (as measured by the consumer price index). At that rate, it takes approximately one hundred years for money to double. Most of us don't have that long to wait. The rate of return for the last thirty-five years is 1.30 percent after inflation. Thus, that is the biggest problem with safe fixed income investments; they do little to protect investors from the depreciation of the purchasing power of the dollar.

What fixed income investments do well, however, is protect the principle of our investments from short-term declines. This makes them useful for emergency funds and short-term goals. They are also useful in our portfolio as the one vehicle that will always go up. In the last thirty-five years, T-bills have *never* had a negative year. The usefulness of this trait will become apparent when I talk about the benefits of portfolio re-balancing in the next chapter.

Treasury Bonds:

The next basic asset category is Treasury bonds. Treasury bonds (or T-bonds) are issued when the government borrows money for ten to thirty years. Because an investor is locking up money for a greater amount of time with T-bonds, they are prone to interest rate risk. If interest rates go up, bond prices go down to compensate. In our thirty-five year period example, T-bonds delivered negative returns in nine of those years. The biggest decline occurred in 1999 when T-bonds lost almost nine percent.

Since the borrower is the same entity with T-bills and T-bonds, we have a good laboratory to view the risk/return trade-off. Since there is more risk with T-bonds, we expect that the rate of return should be higher; and, in fact, this is exactly what we observe. T-bonds outpaced inflation by 3.96 percent over our thirty-five-year period. It is the same borrower, but they must pay more interest in order to get investors to take the increased risk.

One of the helpful aspects of T-bonds is that they have a tendency to move in dissimilar fashion with the stock market. Treasuries often rally when the market goes down, because despite the potential short-term volatility of T-Bonds, investors are assured of getting their money back when the bond matures. This dissimilar price movement helps dampen the volatility of portfolios.

Large U.S. Stocks:

This asset class needs almost no explanation. Large U.S. stocks are a favorite among American investors. After all, these are the companies we read about every day in the news. These would include companies like Apple, IBM, GE, etc.

The past 10 years produced a 7.6% annualized return for the Dow Jones Industrial Average (period ending September 30, 2012). And as you know, it came with a lot of volatility!

Large International Stocks:

The returns are similar because the risks are similar. Large international company returns range from almost seventy percent on the high end to a little over -23 percent on the low end. Many large international firms operate all over the world, just as big U.S. companies operate multi-nationally.

The Vanguard International Fund returned a little over 9% for the 10 year period ending September 30, 2012. This fund has more volatility than that of the Dow Jones Industrial Average.

They tend to be well-run companies that vigorously compete with one another. Many of these companies are household names such as: Nestle, Bayer, Nokia, Toyota, BP, Roche, and Manulife.

Despite the similar risks and returns of large international and large U.S. stocks, these large international companies don't always move in tandem with large U.S. companies. One of the reasons is that significant amounts of manufacturing activity take place outside of the U.S., just as the U.S. begins to lean more and more toward being a service economy. Another reason has to do with exchange rate risk between the dollar and other currencies. If the dollar drops in value verses other currencies, international stocks increase in value in America. That's because it takes more dollars to buy those international entities. The opposite is also true. These factors add to the allure of holding international stocks, because they help diversify by providing more dissimilar price movement within the portfolio; and that tends to reduce risk.

Small U.S. Stocks:

Small U.S. stocks have provided even greater returns than large U.S. stocks throughout time. The Russell 2000 has been up over 13% annualized for the past 10 years ending September 30, 2012. Small companies tend to move differently from large U.S. companies because they are typically more regional in focus. Many small U.S. companies never venture outside the United States when searching for customers. In addition, small companies can often implement new technology much faster than their large company counterparts. They often change direction faster as well, because there is commonly less bureaucracy.

That said, there can also be more volatility with small stocks. Where U.S. large companies dropped twenty-six percent in 1974, small U.S. companies went down over thirty-eight percent the year before. They have also gone through greater upside volatility as well. In 2003, small U.S. stocks shot up over seventy-eight percent. As with the other asset classes mentioned, small companies can serve to dampen volatility, because they don't usually move in lock step with other areas of the market. For instance, in 1998 small U.S. stock went down eight percent while large U.S. companies went up over twenty-eight percent. In 2001, the reverse was true. Large companies dropped almost twelve percent, but small companies jumped almost thirty-four percent.

Small International Stocks:

Just as small U.S. companies tend to outpace large U.S. companies over time, small international companies can have higher returns than their large international counterparts. The Vanguard Small Company Fund averaged over 15% for the period of 10 years, ending September 30, 2012. American investors are often reluctant to add this group of stocks to their portfolios, because they represent a group of stocks that many of us have never even heard of (nor can we pronounce the names of many of them), and because it seems that owning them would drastically increase the risk of our portfolios.

However, research in portfolio design actually shows that we can reduce risk by adding small international stocks to the asset allocation mix.

Now we know the basics about each asset category. As mentioned earlier, the only predictable thing about which asset category will do well is that the answer is unpredictable. That is why it is imperative to spread the wealth across multiple assets.

In the next chapter, I'll use the information about each category to show you how to make proper asset allocations that build a strong investment foundation.

I am not recommending any of the funds listed in this chapter. These funds are to compare indexes of large, small, and international funds.

As you can see, the more risk, the higher return. But with the higher risk comes higher volatility.

You should not 'chase' returns if you have a low risk tolerance.

Investment Success (Part 2)

We've now seen that the lack of investor confidence places some serious obstacles in the way of portfolio success. So how do we remedy that? And what is the only lasting way to gain confidence in your investment decisions? The answer is simple: Become educated. Many of the nervous, unconfident investors are that way simply because they lack basic knowledge of the concepts and principles of investing, thus becoming easy targets for investing myths, clever fund marketing, and Wall Street scare tactics. And by now you know that education is what this book is all about.

In the last chapter, I talked about the foundations of investment success; but we've only laid the first few bricks. We can't build a lasting foundation without knowing the how behind concepts and terminology. Without the how, they're all just a bunch of meaningless words. Now we'll take the asset categories and show that proper asset allocation is not gut feelings and guesswork. There is a science to it. Is it an exact science?   No. But the proven theories in place can help give you real direction, and ultimately, provide you with the confidence you need to tune out the Wall Street marketing machine and invest without fear.

A "Noble" Calling

The Efficient Frontier is a graph that represents portfolio mixes where the level of expected return is highest for a given level of risk that an investor is willing to take.

I often hear investment advisors say that they devise every portfolio differently, because every investor is different. But that idea is nonsense. All investors basically want as much return as they can get for the select amount of volatility they can stomach, so they really aren't all that different.

To explain the concept of the Efficient Frontier, let's say that an investor put all of his money into a fund that tracked the S&P 500 index. An investor could diversify the portfolio more broadly and pick up greater expected return for the risk he takes. Alternatively, if the investor is not comfortable with the risk of owning the S&P 500 stocks, he or she could reallocate his mix and pick up a similar expected return, but with a fraction of the risk.

The "How" Behind the Theory

The how behind the Efficient Frontier is based on an idea to which I have alluded; that is, the different asset classes move in dissimilar fashion with one another. Therefore, putting them together in a portfolio causes the whole to be less risky than the parts.

According to our perfect scenario, when one investment zigs, the other zags. Of course, this isn't always possible. If it were, we could create extremely high returning portfolios with no risk; and, it would make the use of advisors obsolete. The best we can hope for is to have the asset classes move differently enough to reduce the risk we experience. This is actually what tends to happen with portfolios designed in this manner. The reason is that portfolios are brought back to their target allocations on a regular basis. In English, this means that the above portfolio would be re-allocated back to a 50/50 mix anytime it got too far out of balance. If investment A does poorly, but investment B does well, the fund manager would sell some of B and buy more of A. It is simply a matter of making sure your portfolio mix doesn't change drastically. It must remain true to your original intentions.

It is similar to what I described earlier, as being a "contrarian" unpurpose.

That idea may sound like hearsay, because most people are driven to sell the losers in their portfolios and buy more of the winners, but remember the golden rule of investing (and no, it's not, "Whoever has the gold rules."): Buy low and sell high. This may appear to be market timing, but it isn't, as long as it is done on a disciplined basis and not in response to our feelings about what we think may happen in the future.

As an example of how this works, look at the time period from 1988 to 2002. Large U.S. stocks and small U.S. stocks had the same exact return during that time period of 11.5 percent. A hypothetical investment of $50,000 dollars in a non-taxable portfolio would have grown to $255,000 dollars in either area of the market. Investing in both would have yielded $510,000 dollars.

If you put them together, however, and re-balanced annually, the new portfolio would have grown to approximately $543,000 dollars. That's a difference of $33,000 dollars. As a side benefit, the new portfolio as a whole was less volatile (as measured by standard deviation) than the parts.

The Re-balancing Act

Re-balancing your portfolio isn't just something you do annually no matter what. In fact, I don't typically recommend re-balancing your allocation unless your portfolio is deviating from your target percentages by twenty-five percent or more. In other words, if you have two different asset categories that should each be taking up ten percent of your portfolio, it is not necessary to re-balance unless one of them is now at 12.5 percent or 7.5 percent (25 percent of 10 percent is 2.5 percent).

Another way to re-balance is to make sure that money you add to the portfolio goes into the areas that are under-represented. Of course, you should do the opposite when pulling money out by withdrawing it from the areas that are over-represented. Re-balancing may have to be tailored for your tax circumstances as well. If the re-balance will trigger unwanted taxes, then it may be best to wait for a more opportune time. As you can see, this is not for the faint of heart and may be best left to professionals.

The Three Factor Model

What else explains the higher return we may expect from more diversified portfolios? One of the most important discoveries in modern investment research is a concept called the Fama-French Three Factor Model. Developed by Eugene Fama and Kenneth French, their model explains that there are three factors responsible for approximately ninety-five percent of the levels of returns you can expect from a portfolio. By changing how much exposure you have to these factors, you can change the expected return of the portfolio. This will also alter the amount of risk. The three factors considered in the model are: 1) Stocks vs. Bonds 2) Small Companies vs. Large Companies and 3) Value Stocks vs. Growth Stocks.

1. Stocks vs. Bonds

The first factor of the Three Factor Model is the comparison of stocks versus bonds, which is often referred to as the market factor. As you know, stocks tend to outperform bonds over the long run, but stocks are obviously more risky. In fact, from 1926 until 2007, one-month treasury bills averaged 3.73 percent with a standard deviation of 3.09—both low risk and low return. Stocks during that time period (as measured by the S&P 500) had a return of 10.36 percent with a standard deviation of 19.97—both higher risk and higher return.

2. Small Companies vs. Large Companies

Just as stocks tend to deliver higher returns over time, small companies tend to display higher returns than large companies. This return difference is also the result of the increased volatility of the small company asset category. Small companies tend to be less immune to economic fluctuations and are more prone to financial difficulty. From

1926 to 2007, small stocks delivered returns of 12.49 percent with a much higher standard deviation of 38.83.

You may be wondering how small a company has to be to be considered small. Well, much of the research about stock returns and the data used in this book comes from the University of Chicago Center for Research in Security Prices (CRSP). The database actually breaks the market up into tenths or deciles. For example, decile one includes the largest ten percent of companies listed on the New York Stock Exchange as well as all like-size companies on the other exchanges. The database defines small companies as belonging to deciles nine through ten, which are the smallest twenty percent of the companies in the CRSP database.

Since companies generally grow, you can see how this makes "small" a moving target. To keep it simple, when searching for small company stock, I generally look for funds that hold stocks whose average market capitalization is less than one billion.

3. Value Stocks vs. Growth Stocks

The third factor of the Three Factor Model is the one that surprises most investors. It is based on the same logic as the previous two, but because of the indoctrination of investors at the hand of the investment industry, at first blush it doesn't seem to make sense. This factor says that value stocks tend to outperform growth stocks. In other words, this means that distressed companies tend to have higher returns than strong and stable companies. This is surprising because most of us believe that the financial advisor's job is to make sure we own nothing but great companies in our portfolios.

If you compare great companies to poorly run companies, great companies seem to win in every area of financial analysis. They often have better asset growth, equity growth, return on total capital, return on equity, and return on sales. Despite this fact, the returns that investors receive from buying these distressed stocks are often much higher than their healthy counterparts. The reason is largely because investors aren't willing to pay as much for each dollar of earnings that a distressed company generates; therefore, any improvement in the operation of the company can cause a big climb in the stock's price.

I use an analogy from the world of golf to make this point. It starts by asking the question, "Who is a better golfer—Tiger Woods or Ken Mahoney?" Most of my clients will quickly say "Tiger." Then I ask a second question. "Who has a better shot of knocking ten strokes off of his score?" Now the answer becomes "Ken." All I have to do is hire a golf instructor for about an hour to discover a few secrets to improve my game and my score; but Tiger has already honed his game to peak efficiency.

It is the same for well-run companies. They are doing many of the things that make a company great, and their stock prices already reflect the fact that investors recognize their efforts. It is the companies that are not well run that have all the room for improvement.

I am not suggesting you go out and buy companies near default. I wanted to stress the results of a long-term study that I found very interesting.

Value Companies Defined

Determining whether a mutual fund is truly investing in value companies can become ridiculously complex. Even experienced financial professionals sometimes have a hard time figuring out which funds are truly focused on value stocks as defined by the Fama-French research.

There are a several ways to define value companies in the investing world, so it's not as easy as looking at the fund's name to determine if it is truly focused on buying value stocks. A mutual fund may be called the ABC Value fund but not really own any value stocks by the Fama-French definition. One way to determine if this is the case is to look at the objective of the fund in the fund prospectus. You may see that the goal of the fund manager is to find mispriced stocks that are supposedly a "value" on the stock market. This is a why many in the academic community don't like the word "value," because the term leads one to think that something is selling for less than it is worth. As we discussed, the market already does a pretty good job of making sure that pricing imperfections get eliminated; so big bargains aren't necessarily just sitting out there waiting for a better-informed investor to sniff them out.

Other ways to define value revolve around the use of statistical measures and key financial ratios. Three commonly used ratios to identify value are: Price to

Earnings, Price to Sales, and Price to Book. As you can see, all three ratios compare the company's current stock price to another important financial number. In the Fama-French research, they used only one of those ratios to define value—Price to Book. The reason is that the other two ratios don't have a stable denominator. In other words, the other two ratio's denominators—Earnings and Sales—may fluctuate quite a bit from one year to the next in a company, but a company's Book Value (assets minus liabilities) tends to be more stable over time. This can be important, because it would make no sense if stocks jumped in and out of the Value category on a frequent basis. Companies don't move in and out of distress in a rapid manner.

Further, the Fama-French research defined value companies as those companies who's Price to Book fell into the bottom thirty percent of all companies listed on the New York Stock Exchange. (Technically, they used the inverse of the ratio in their research, Book to Market.) It makes sense if you think about it. A company that is selling at or near the value of its assets minus what it owes (its liabilities) must be in some distress or investors would place a higher value on it.

Staying Ahead

You may be faced with the challenge of picking a value fund in your 401(k) or other such retirement plan. In that case, you are probably looking for an easy way to implement the information laid out in this chapter. Unfortunately, there is no easy or foolproof system to make sure that the fund you choose is a great value fund. The ratios that define value stocks are moving targets as the investing climate changes.

More often than not, a 401(k) plan won't even have a fund that truly meets any of the criteria we just discussed.

So what do you do? For one, you can look at the selections called value and try to select the ones containing stocks with lower Price to Book ratios. You can also utilize a useful tool called the Morningstar Style Box. The Style Box attempts to classify mutual funds in nine different areas: Large Growth, Large Blend, Large Value, Mid-Cap Growth, Mid-Cap Blend, Mid-Cap Value, Small Growth, Small Blend, and Small Value. Although their definition of value varies slightly from the one used above, it can be helpful as a starting point for choosing funds for your mix.

Keep in mind that these guidelines are rough at best.

Knowing that your mix of assets is the most important thing upon which you should focus gives you permission to ignore all of the noise made by the investing industry. You can ignore all of the hype about which stocks to buy, when to get in the market, when to get out, and what the Fed is going to do next. The key idea is that you can set up your portfolio mix based on your goals and then just maintain the mix through re-balancing.

Using Fama and French's three factors is kind of like finger painting. If you take yellow and blue and mix them, you know you'll get green. The more yellow you add, the lighter the resulting shade of green. Changing exposure to these different factors can increase or decrease the expected returns and risk of your portfolio depending on what you want to accomplish.

Asset Allocation, (Re-) Balancing and You

Because baby boomers are living longer than the generations before them, the United States Labor Department recommends that baby boomers plan for a 30-years' worth of income to cover their expenses during retirement. This helps boomers to ensure that they don't run out of money before they die. Your financial affairs are not going to organize and plan themselves, which means you need to be proactive in planning for your retirement.

Getting your financial future in focus requires taking steps to understand the state of your finances today and to make a plan for what kind of income and expenses you will have during retirement. Once you have these figures, you will be able to plan out the steps you need to take now in order to get you to where you need to be for retirement. It does not end there either. It is not a plan you create and walk away from for 30 years until you are ready to retire. Your retirement plan requires you to regularly review your financial investments to see how each one is performing and make necessary adjustments as time goes by.

Risk

Risk is something you need to adjust as the years go by. When you are in your 20's, you have forty years or so for your investments to grow before you retire. You have the time to take on more risk when choosing investments in your 20's than you do in your 40's when you only have 20 years or so until retirement.

Even during your retirement years, your risk level changes, decreasing more and more as you get further and further into your retirement.

Asset Allocation

When people think about retirement, a lot of times they make the mistake of thinking about things one way. Okay, I have a pension, or maybe I'll just have Social Security. When you think about a stool or a chair, the more legs it has, the steadier it's going to be, right? So you can't imagine a one-legged chair, because it would fall over.

When you think about retirement, I want you to think about different legs you can have, the different sources of income that provide your retirement. You may have a pension. You may have Social Security. You may have investments which produce income. You may have a small business, or a real estate interest that produces income. Now, think about your chair having many legs to support it. Once you visualize that, you'll realize that it will work out a lot better if you have four or five legs. If one breaks off, let's say your investments or real estate doesn't work as well, you still have other legs to support that chair. Think about retirement visually. Rather than relying on one source of income to produce what you need for retirement, you rely on many different sources, so you are prepared for the worst.

It's extremely important to diversify your retirement investment portfolio. Diversification helps you to balance your portfolio, so when one investment is not doing well, the other investments that are doing well balance the portfolio out—reducing your losses. Once you have a clear sense of your current asset allocation, it is also important to remember that you have to be flexible—even as the years pass away. Flexibility is important because it will allow you to make clear and educated choices on changes that you need to make in your portfolio to get your investments back on track—helping you to reach your retirement goals.

Types of Investments

Everyone is different and investment needs are just as different as people. Luckily, there are many different investment possibilities to choose from; which means you can look for and invest in investment vehicles that are right for you.

- Passbook Savings Accounts
- Certificates of Deposit (CDs)
- Real Estate
- Stocks
- Bonds
- Mutual Funds
- Precious Metals and Commodities
- Foreign currencies
- Annuities

Investment Rule Of Thumb

The rule of thumb used to keep financial portfolios balanced is to deduct your current age from 100. The answer you get is the percentage of your portfolio that might be invested in stocks. The remaining percentage should be invested in bonds and cash. So if you are 40 years old now, 60% of your retirement investment portfolio should be invested in a variety of stocks. The remaining 40% of your portfolio should be in bonds and cash.

There are a lot more variables that go into what percentage should be in stocks then just age.

Why this rule? It goes back to the thought process of asset allocation, which states that as we get older, we should take less risk. Since stocks tend to be volatile, while bonds and cash are more stable, it makes sense that the older we get the more we will reallocate the stock investments in our portfolio into cash and bonds—the safer investments. A stock heavy portfolio can leave you with big losses, which can wreak financial havoc on your retirement when you need to sell or liquidate the stocks for income.

On the flipside, cash and bonds are victims of inflation. These investments usually do not grow at a value that keeps up with or is higher than the inflation rate. For example, cash and bonds may grow at a rate of 2% per year and inflation may increase by 4% per year. In this type of a scenario, your portfolio is not growing enough to cover the costs. So while you may decrease the risk of capital losses by limiting the percentage of your stock investments as time goes by, you can decrease your buying power as inflation eats away at your cash and bond earnings. This is why it is important to find a balance in the investments in your retirement portfolio.

Assessing Your Situation

Nobody knows you better than you. Think about how you tend to deal with things, what your risk tolerance is, and how you handle making decisions. After you assess yourself in these areas, it helps you to better manage and allocate your assets. You spend all of your life trying to earn as much income as you can and are willing and able to take on risks—changing jobs, higher investment risk, etc. When retirement strikes the role reverses and you have to take on less risk and may not have the opportunity to earn as much income as you did during your working years. This does not mean that now that you are retired you can just sit back with your feet up and let your investment portfolio unwind. Even during your retirement you have to manage your investments—reviewing, re-evaluating, and reallocating when necessary.

Most people know that the trick to making money in the investment arena is to buy low and sell high. So why do "real people" end up buying high and selling low? It's what is referred to as the "bandwagon" effect. When stocks, bonds, and real estate are increasing in value, the adrenaline flows and everyone, except for maybe Warren Buffet and a few others, wants to jump on the bandwagon and make a killing, so they buy high. Fortunately or unfortunately, the market is a constantly changing entity, so when the market takes a turn for the worse, investors panic and sell off their investments just as the market is bottoming out. And when the market makes an upward turn, the confidence of investors is restored and they begin investing in the market—buying investments at a higher price. This phenomenon creates a situation where investors pay the most to buy or purchase the investment, and lose the most when they sell.

Balancing and Re-Balancing Your Portfolio

In its simplest terms, balancing your portfolio means keeping a pre-determined percentage of stocks, bonds, cash and other equities in your retirement account.

Re-balancing your portfolio means selling off some assets that have gained value and replacing them by buying some less expensive investments or those that have become less expensive. You may wonder why, if your portfolio is doing great, you would want to re-balance.

Here's why...

Let's assume you diversified your $100,000 portfolio in accordance with the following predetermined balance of stocks, bonds, and cash.

Stocks 50% $50,000
Bonds 40% $40,000
Cash   10% $10,000

Total 100% $100,000

Now, let's pretend the market has been very good to you and your portfolio currently looks like this:

Stocks 60% $ 72,000
Bonds 35% $ 42,000
Cash   5% $ 6,000
Total 100% $120,000

You're ecstatic! And you should be – you've made $20,000!

No doubt, you're very pleased with yourself and are already dreaming of what to do with all that profit. Unfortunately, there are problems with your fantasy of your newfound riches. To begin with, you have not really made a profit because you haven't sold your stock--turning it into money. And your $20,000 gain has moved you away from your original asset allocation plan, which exposes you to greater financial risk.

If your original decision to balance your portfolio with 50% in stocks was a sound decision, there is good reason not to change it now. Just remembering the '.com' crashes of 2000 will confirm this theory. Before the .com market crashed, many investors' portfolios were so highly concentrated with technology stocks that when the technology sector was doing great, these stock portfolios skyrocketed. Investors tend to 'chase' performance as I mentioned earlier. But when the technology sector tanked, which happened practically overnight, these portfolios went right down the drain with it. Since these portfolios were not diversified or re-allocated as the value of the portfolio increased, the investors did not have any other stocks to fall back on to balance the bad performing stocks with some good performers.

Investopedia.com defines portfolio re-balancing as "the process of realigning the weightings of one's portfolio of assets." In other words, you do something with that $20,000 so that your portfolio is divided along the same percentages that you planned for when you began building your portfolio. You can take the money you gained and invest it into bond holdings and cash as you get closer to retirement, so that you get your portfolio allocation plan back to your original percentages. By doing it this way, you can make a great deal of money with very little risk!

When to Re-balance

The general rule of thumb is that you should re-balance your asset allocation when your assets drift 5% or more away from your original allocation plan. A portfolio that is too heavily weighted in one area can be dangerous because the economy moves in cycles, which means your stock holdings could end up plunging so deeply that moving your portfolio back to its original allotment might take years, or might never happen.

Example: Tim Middleton, in his MSN article Spring Training for Your Portfolio in February 2007, compares portfolio re-balancing to bunting in baseball. By re-balancing you may not knock the ball out of the park, but by making small adjustments you'll gradually move your assets toward home plate, and eventually you'll score that big winning run.

Re-balancing helps take the emotion out of investing also. Instead of following the herd and selling when others are selling, or buying when everyone else is buying, you can become a contrarian—a maverick investor.

That is, you can zig while the market zags and vice versa. So often, when the market or an industry is doing poorly, there are panic sell offs by those with "weak stomachs." This is the time when "long-term" investors, like Warren Buffet, step in and buy up the bargains.

While re-balancing is not a guarantee against loss, it:

- Ensures that you'll be buying low and selling high
- Reduces volatility in your portfolio
- Gives you a sense of consistency
- Offers a process in which emotion and guesswork are eliminated

Where to Retire to

"No matter where you go, there you are." I hope you don't travel too far from Mahoney Asset Management when you retire, we will miss you! But if you do want to leave this area because of higher costs of housing, taxes, etc. (everything), this is a list I came up with after many years of what clients, friends (and articles) shared.

1. *Santa Fe, New Mexico*

Joel Stein, a corporate bond broker from New York City, and his wife retired to Santa Fe in 1997. The reason: "It's like a microcosm of New York but without the hustle and bustle," he says. "It's a small town but it's sophisticated -- there's art, opera and hundreds of restaurants. It's a nice place to retire to but it doesn't feel like a 'retirement town'."

Nicknamed "City Different," Santa Fe is indeed unlike the trendier Sedona, an Arizona town that's often touted as one of the best places to retire. Unemployment is just 5.3%, thanks to the city's thriving tourism business and government payroll. (Santa Fe is the state capital.)

The arts scene is one of the best you'll find anywhere. The city is dotted with 240 art galleries and is the home of Art Santa Fe, an international art fair that attracts buyers and tourists from around the globe. In fact, according to the University of New Mexico Bureau of Business and Economic Research, Santa Fe's art market is the fourth largest in the country in terms of sales. Stein says he and his wife have embraced the scene. He leads historic walking tours of the area and works for pay at the Museum of Natural History; she is a docent at a local art museum.

For retirees who want to work, tourism-related jobs are a good bet, says Steve Lewis, a spokesperson for the Santa Fe Convention & Visitor's Bureau. In addition, many people retire here to reinvent themselves. "We get a lot of people who have always wanted to be artists, and they come here to do it," he adds.

Medical and travel information: The Christus St. Vincent Regional Medicare Center, which is the regional medical center for northern New Mexico, is in Santa Fe. The Albuquerque airport, which serves 10 major airlines, is about an hour drive.

Climate is warm with low humidity and little rain.

	Santa Fe, NM	Sedona, AZ
Cost of living compared to national average	17.9% higher	36.8% higher
State tax rate	1.7% - 4.9%	2.59% - 4.54%
Median home sales price	$225,852*	$349,700
Unemployment rate*	5.3%	7.9%**, 10%***

* Zillow real estate data not available for Santa Fe, so Trulia data used here.
** The unemployment rate for Flagstaff, AZ, the closest major locale, 30 miles from Sedona.
*** The unemployment rate in Sedona proper, according to Sperling's Best Places.

2. *Lincoln, Nebraska*

Lincoln is the quintessential Midwestern town -- friendly people, college football and picturesque landscapes. Residents take a brimming pride in their city's low crime rate and accessible natural beauty, including ten nearby lakes and more than 99 miles of recreational trails.

Lincoln sounds a lot like another Midwest retirement haven that frequents the best lists: Ann Arbor, Michigan. But Nebraska's state capital has a much lower unemployment rate, just 3.6% compared to Ann Arbor's 7.2%.

Even more surprising, especially for a Midwest town, is that in the past two decades the jobless rate in this state capital has never gone above 5%, according to the Bureau of Labor Statistics. The University of Nebraska, government jobs, as well a sizable corporate presence, including Kawasaki and Assurity Life Insurance, help keep employment stable. And Lincoln is affordable: Housing prices have remained relatively flat since 2007, with a two-bedroom home now running for about $115,000.

No wonder Jim Strand, a 65-year-old Lincoln resident, decided to stay put when he quit working. "Stability is really important with all the craziness in the financial and housing markets," he says. Strand, who served as the interim business manager for the local zoo for the first eight months of this year, appreciates the job and volunteer opportunities: "It's nice to feel like you are part of the community."

Medical and travel information: There are three major hospitals in Lincoln. The local airport offers direct flights to most major cities in America via Delta or United.

Seasonal climates can include extreme heat during the summer months and extreme cold during winter months.

	Lincoln, NE	Ann Arbor, MI
Cost of living compared to national average	6.7% lower	60% higher
State tax rate	2.56% - 6.84%	4.35%
Median home sales price	$135,200	$214,600
Unemployment rate*	3.6%	7.2%

3.   Manhattan, Kansas

The Little Apple, as Manhattan, Kansas is known, is perfect for active, outdoorsy retirees who also want the cultural and educational opportunities that a college town brings. The 1,200 acre Tuttle Creek Park boasts a 12,500 acre reservoir and 100 miles of shoreline with walking paths. The Flint Hills nature preserve (yes, there are hills in Kansas) is the last large tract of protected prairie land in North America. After a day spent enjoying nature, residents can reward themselves with dinner out at one of the towns 130 restaurants.

Retirees can take or audit dozens of classes -- from Martial Arts to Spanish -- at the UFM Community Learning Center or at Kansas State University. Manhattan actually conjures up images of retirement hotspot Athens, Georgia -- another college town with an abundance of good restaurants and outdoorsy activities.

Here's the difference: Manhattan, Kansas, is a cheaper place to live. The cost of living is almost 9% lower than the national average and the lowest on our list of cities. (Athens has a cost of living that is just 3.9% lower than average.) Unemployment is also low, coming in at 5.9%.

For boomers dreaming of an entrepreneurial second act, Manhattan is a great place to open a store or other small business. The 23,000 students attending Kansas State University and the personnel at Fort Riley Army base help keeps the local economy humming. Better yet, experts say commercial real estate is a bargain -- retail space rents in the $20-25 per square foot range -- and retail sales in the area have increased about 66% in the past decade, according to John Pagen, Vice President for the Chamber of Commerce.

Meanwhile, the Department of Homeland Security is building a $720 million National Bio and Agro-Defense Facility, due to be completed by 2018. When that opens, the local economy will likely get another boost.

Medical and travel information: The city is served by Mercy Regional Hospital. A small local airport offers direct flights to Dallas and Chicago.

Seasonal temperatures can be extreme in winter and summer months.

	Manhattan, KS	Athens, GA
Cost of living compared to national average	8.9% lower	3.9% lower

State tax rate	3.5% - 6.45%	1% - 6%
Median home sales price	$152,200*	$144,900
Unemployment rate*	5.9%	7.8%

* Data from Zillow and Trulia not available, so this data is from Sperlings Best Places.

4.   *Portland, Maine*

Northampton, Massachusetts lands at the top of many "best places to retire" lists. And for good reason: It's a scenic mountain town with lots of Berkshire culture. It's also home to Smith College and is close to four other name schools. But charm comes at a price -- it costs nearly 20% more than the average city to live there.

Head about 200 miles north and you'll hit Portland, Maine, where the culture and natural beauty rivals Northampton thanks to miles of coastline, the popular fishing area of Sebago Lake, which is only a short drive from the city, and a smattering of islands around the coast. "Portland is known for its natural beauty," says travel blogger Lee Abbamonte.

Foodies also take note: Bon Appétit recently rated the city as one of the top small towns in America, due in part to some notable chefs. Hugo's, for example, is run by French Laundry chef Rob Evans and the chef at Fore Street is a James Beard Foundation Award winner, one of the most prestigious culinary awards.

Portland offers all this and incredible value for money. Homes here are about 44% less expensive than in Northampton -- and right around the median price for a home nationwide. Unemployment is well below the national average, with many big employers such as Maine Medical Center, the largest hospital in the state, TD Bank and, of course, clothing company L.L. Bean. With its steady population growth and relatively low commercial real estate costs, Portland often ranks as one of the best places to start a small business, and deservedly so.

Medical and travel information: There are two major hospitals in the Portland area. A major airport offers flights to most U.S. Cities.

Typical New England seasonal climate can produce hot summers and cold winters with a good chance of snow.

	Portland, ME	Northampton, MA
Cost of living compared to national average	10% higher	19.8% higher
State tax rate	2% - 8.5%	5.30%
Median home sales price	$179,500	$320,000
Unemployment rate*	5.2%	5.3%, 8.4%

* 5.3% reflects the unemployment rate for only the small town of Northampton (data is from Sperling's Best Places). 8.4% is data from the Bureau of Labor Statistics and reflects the unemployment rate for nearby Springfield, the closest city.

5.   *Santa Maria, California*

California's Sonoma and Napa counties have long been the gold standard of California wine country and a Mecca for retirees. But prices have risen with that popularity. The median home price in Sonoma County's Santa Rosa, for instance, is close to $300,000, and the cost of living is 45% above average. High prices like these are encouraging Chardonnay-sipping retirees to look at some of the less popular, more affordable corners of wine country.

Santa Maria is one such gem, says Warren Bland, the author of "Retire in Style: 60 Outstanding Places across the USA and Canada." Part of the Santa Barbara wine region, which produces highly rated Chardonnays and Pinot Noirs, Santa Maria residents enjoy temperatures in the 60s and 70s nearly year around and little rain. And while the local job market isn't exactly buzzing, nearby San Luis Obispo (just 30 miles away) and Santa Barbara (75 miles away) have healthier job markets than most California cities and are within driving distance.

Three years ago, when 82-year-old Jack Pellerin from Santa Ynez married a woman from Santa Maria, the couple realized they had too much stuff to fit into one house. So they decided they'd keep both places, splitting their time between them. Soon after, Santa Maria's charms won the couple over to the point where they are almost full-time residents. "It's just the right size -- it's big enough that you can get involved in a lot of things, but you still know a lot of people," says Pellerin. The best part, they say: Santa Maria isn't overrun with tourists.

Medical and travel information: The brand-new Marin Hospital is located in Santa Maria, with several larger hospitals in nearby San Luis Obispo. A major airport is also located in San Luis Obispo.

Typical west coast climate includes hot summers and mild winters.

	Santa Maria, CA	Santa Rosa, CA
Cost of living compared to national average	20% higher	44.8% higher
State tax rate	1% - 9.3%	1% - 9.3%
Median home sales price	$230,900	$294,300
Unemployment rate*	8.8%*	10%**

* 8.8% reflects the unemployment rate for the Santa Barbra/Santa Maria/Goleta area
** 10% reflects the unemployment rate for the Santa Rosa/Petaluma area

6. Jupiter, Florida

The Great Recession took a heavy toll on Florida. Unemployment stands at 11% and median home sales prices have plummeted more than 40% since early 2007. Unfortunately that didn't create loads of housing bargains in some of Florida's most popular retirement spots, many of which were overvalued when the recession began. In Naples, for instance, the median home price is still half a million bucks, according to Zillow.com, even though prices dropped roughly 35% from their highs in early 2007.

While some of Florida's posh areas may still be unaffordable for many retirees, lower home prices in other parts of the state have created some attractive alternatives. Jupiter, for instance, on Florida's Atlantic-facing "Gold Coast", offers similar pristine beaches, year-round warm weather, golf courses and shopping in Naples, but is about half the price to live in, according to data from Sperling's Best Places. The award-winning, 600-seat Maltz Jupiter Theatre, a regional theater that hosts well-known shows like Cabaret and Hello Dolly! as well as smaller shows, is a bonus, and swanky Palm Beach is only a 30 minute drive for those who want to stroll through the lap of luxury without having to pay for it.

As for job opportunities, an unemployment rate of 8% means Jupiter fares better than most of Florida. The area benefits from hosting the spring training seasons for two professional baseball teams, the Florida Marlins and the St. Louis Cardinals, as well as biotech companies like the Scripps Institute and the Max Planck Society.

Medical and travel information: Jupiter Medical Center and several major hospitals in the Palm Beach area. Palm Beach International Airport offers direct flights to U.S. and international cities.

	Jupiter, FL	Naples, FL
Cost of living compared to national average	21.3% higher	84% higher
State tax rate	None	None
Median home sales price	$238,200	$527,300
Unemployment rate*	8.2%*	11.9%, 10%**

* The 8.2% rate is from Sperling's Best Places since data from the Bureau of Labor Statistics was not available for the area.
** The 11.9% figure is for the Naples/Marco Island area from the Bureau of Labor of Statistics; the 10% figure is from Sperling's Best Places and is just for Naples.

7.   *Ithaca, New York*

When the Dalai Lama decided to put down roots in the United States, he didn't opt for Buddhist-heavy San Francisco or Eugene, Oregon, with their many meditation-loving residents. Instead, he came to Ithaca, New York, to "offer Western students the opportunity to study authentic Tibetan Buddhism in a monastic setting."

That doesn't surprise many of Ithaca's 30,000 residents. "It's one of the loveliest places in America," says 76-year-old Roger Battistella, a retired Cornell college professor. The town is known for its beauty: you'll find dozens of waterfalls and craggy gorges that gave rise to tacky bumper stickers and t-shirts that sport the now ubiquitous "Ithaca is Gorges" tagline. But that doesn't spoil the area's 25,000 acres of national forest or the 40-mile long Cayuga Lake.

Perhaps it's all this beauty that gives Ithaca its liberal, beatnik bent. "There's a zany political culture here," says Battistella. The "world's largest human peace sign" was created in Ithaca, when a local teen activist gathered nearly 6,000 people in 2008. Residents are well-versed in the art of protesting, as evidenced by recent Occupy Wall Street events and a rally in front of a local Bank of America branch. Ithaca brings to mind another popular retirement town: Eugene, Oregon. True, the towns are nearly 3,000 miles apart and on opposite coasts, but both are havens for activist, outdoorsy retirees.

In Ithaca, your money goes farther -- it's about 13% cheaper to live in Ithaca than Eugene -- and you've got a better chance of landing a job. The unemployment rate is just 5.8%, well below the national average.

One of the reasons for Ithaca's low unemployment is the presence of two highly rated universities, Cornell University and Ithaca College. And it's not just young people who land jobs there: AARP has named Cornell one of the top employers for people over 50, particularly in the green technology and tourism industries. And there are plenty of non-work related things to do. This past semester you could have taken a course on tropical field ornithology (the study of exotic birds), or seen comedian, Jon Stewart in person, or cheered through an ice hockey face-off between Cornell's "Big Red" and Dartmouth's "Big Green."

Don't forget the food, say travel experts: Ithaca has some standout restaurants, including the seminal vegetarian Moosewood Restaurant, which Bon Appétit said was "one of the 13 most influential and revolutionary restaurants of the 20th century."

Medical and travel information: Cayuga Medical Center employs 200 doctors. A small local airport services direct flights to Philadelphia, New York and Detroit. For more direct flights, the Syracuse airport is roughly an hour and a half drive from Ithaca.

	Ithaca, NY	Eugene, OR
Cost of living compared to national average	30% lower	12.2% higher
State tax rate	4% - 9%	5% - 11%
Median home sales price	$189,100	$215,700
Unemployment rate*	5.8%	9.5%

Managing Your Money after Retirement

For much of your life you've focused on accumulating wealth. Perhaps you've been contributing to a 401k, an IRA, and/or a brokerage account – or maybe you purchased an annuity – all without a clear plan or strategy for how to actually use those resources for your maximum benefit.

Now that you've retired or are about to retire, you may develop a deep fear of running out of money. Lots of folks do. And because of that fear, whether conscious or not, they try to hoard what they have, unnecessarily depriving themselves of the retirement life they worked so hard and so long to achieve.

Below are several different strategies for you, so you can effectively, efficiently, and predictably make the best use of your money. You'll learn how to cover your expenses, even as they rise with inflation, with income pooled from tax-deferred as well as after-tax resources.

Keeping Retirement Assets Safe

In finance, there is a concept called "risk of ruin". For a trader, it means the risk of bankruptcy, but for a retiree, it refers to the risk of outliving the profitability of one's assets. A retiree that can produce all the spending money he or she needs for a year, from a cash/fixed income based portfolio, does not need to worry, but a bond or investment based portfolio will face reinvestment based risk as the economy and the financial climate changes over time.

For example, if a high interest-paying bond matures and pays out when interest rates have lowered; buying a new bond to replace it will not generate as much income as before. That will hurt a retired person's wallet, but it will not immediately ruin him or her.

The real risk of ruin for the retired originates in the unpredictable nature of the stock market, as well as the need to liquidate their assets every so often to provide themselves with income to pay the bills. A withdrawal made from a portfolio in a flat market creates risk of ruin, just like that faced by an active trader losing in the markets.

For both, the solution is the same – start out with enough liquid capital to withstand losses, even a string of them. Doing that requires you to weigh the likelihood of future returns against the rate of inflation.

Sequence Counts for More than Rate

Relying on any one period of market performance to guide your retirement decisions is a big mistake. For a retiree, or for anyone who has to make regular withdrawals from his or her portfolio, the sequence of returns proves to be far more important than just the rate.

From 1966 to 1983, a period of seventeen years, the market was flat and facing the highest inflation rate on record. Very few stockbrokers or financial advisors refer to that period of time in their resources and illustrations.

Four percent is the withdrawal rate used or suggested by a great many financial advisors, but it is not a universal guarantee. These numbers are arrived at using average annual returns, which can differ greatly from actual annual returns. Between 1926 and 2007, the Standard & Poor's 500 Index (known as the S&P 500) performance was a gain or a loss of more than twenty percent in 54 out of those 82 years. To break down the math, that means that almost two thirds of the time the S&P index was widely above or below average. The index returned an average 10% return only 33% of the time.

So the average annual return isn't as important as it looks. What *is* important is the *sequence* of returns.

Over the seventeen years between 1987 and 2003, the S&P 500 had an average return of 13.47%. It doesn't make any difference whether you choose to look at the returns from 1987 to 2003 or from 2003 to 1987.

But if you are a retiree making regular withdrawals from your portfolio, the sequence of returns becomes vitally important. You are still working with the exact same initial capital, withdrawal amount and returns, but a different sequence of returns makes for a very different outcome.

In the example of a $100,000 portfolio, with the retiree taking out $10,000 a year, and adjusting for a 4% rate of inflation over 17 years, the difference at the end of the period ranges between a comfortable remaining balance of $76,629 to a staggering deficit of $187,606, all depending on the difference in the sequence of returns. The following table illustrates how this is so.

A New Way To Look At Retirement

Year	Portfolio Value - Beginning of Year	Value After $10,000 Inflation-Adjusted Withdrawal	Rate of Return	Portfolio Value -Year End
1987	100,000	90,000	5.25%	94,725
1988	94,725	84,325	16.61%	98,331
1989	98,331	87,515	31.69%	115,249
1990	115,249	104,000	-3.11%	100,766
1991	100,766	89,067	30.47%	116,206
1992	116,206	104,040	7.62%	111,967
1993	111,967	99,314	10.08%	109,325
1994	109,325	96,166	1.32%	97,435
1995	97,435	83,750	37.58%	115,223
1996	115,223	100,990	22.96%	124,177
1997	124,177	109,374	33.36%	145,862
1998	145,862	130,467	28.58%	167,754
1999	167,754	151,744	21.04%	183,671
2000	183,671	167,020	-9.11%	151,805
2001	151,805	134,488	-11.89%	118,497
2002	118,497	100,488	-22.10%	78,280
2003	78,280	59,550	28.68%	76,629
	Average Annual Return:		**13.47%**	

	Portfolio Value - Beginning of Year	Value After $10,000 Inflation Adjusted Withdrawal	Rate of Return	Portfolio Value - Year End
2003	100,000	90,000	28.68%	115,812
2002	115,812	105,412	-22.10%	82,116
2001	82,116	71,300	-11.89%	62,822
2000	62,822	51,574	-9.11%	46,875
1999	46,875	35,177	21.04%	42,578
1998	42,578	30,411	28.58%	39,103
1997	39,103	26,450	33.36%	35,274
1996	35,274	22,114	22.96%	27,192
1995	27,192	13,506	37.58%	18,581
1994	18,581	4,348	1.32%	4,406
1993	4,406	0	10.08%	0
	Average Annual Return:		**13.47%**	

The most interesting part of this result is that the three consecutive years of negative returns more than completely cancel out the positive returns of five consecutive years of excellent returns. The period between 1995-1999 saw returns of +37.6%, +23.0%, +33.4%, +28.6% and +21.0%, the best bull market anyone had seen in some time, and a 'winning streak' that is unlikely to recur soon.

In spite of five consecutive years of unprecedented returns, the example portfolio drops in value to $4,348 following the tenth year's withdrawal. This is the point of ruin.

How to Avoid Outliving Your Savings and What To Do If You Do

As you can see, the most important issue to a retiree is the market's condition early in retirement. If the market is poor prior to retirement, consider a delay of one or two years to gain more capital and allow time for conditions to improve, which can vastly reduce risk of ruin. If the market worsens during retirement, you may have to take action, either seeking some employment or proportionately reducing your cost of living.

The concept of risk of ruin points to many more concepts that each and every investor should take into consideration before making retirement decisions.

Accumulated capital is vital – Aim to accumulate a good supply of starting capital to absorb potential losses. Beware of investing in anything that advertises itself based only on good performance years.

Focus on periodic returns over cumulative returns – Average returns are less important when you are making withdrawals. What is more important is maximizing the amount of money you will have at each years end to reinvest for profit in the next year.

Minimize fixed costs as much as possible – Keeping your spending needs flexible is the best way to avoid outliving your assets. If your spending is flexible, your income needs are flexible as well, which can be beneficial when the market is down. However, fixed costs reduce flexibility. Retiring while still responsible for a mortgage or other debt imposes a cost that cannot and will not change if your income does, which can sink you in bad market conditions. Work towards no-credit, all cash.

Allocate your assets wisely – Allocate assets and investments to avoid significant losses in a given financial year. "Loss avoidance" is key – take a small loss and get out before it turns into a bigger loss, because both the time and the math are against an investor trying to recoup losses, especially while taking withdrawals. After a 10% loss, an 11% gain makes back the money. However, after a 25% loss, a 33% gain is required to break even. Take care of your investments and favor small losses over big risks.

Conclusion

A long term investor can play a long term game – market risk is a given and long term positive performance makes up for losses in the short term. But a retiree-investor who must routinely liquidate their assets for income can't play on the same terms. The risk of ruin for the retiree-investor is much greater, and so the retiree must know at all times how much of a loss he or she will be able to absorb and still have money left over for the year ahead.

6 Excellent Tips for Making Your Retirement Budget Stretch

The NCHS (National Center for Health Statistics) says that in 1950, life expectancy averaged at 68.2 years of age. By 1970 it was at 70.8 years, and by 2008, it had risen to 78.1 years. People are living longer, but this is only good for them if they are able to maintain a good quality of life. To guarantee yourself a good quality of life throughout your retirement, you have to make sure that you will be able to meet the various financial challenges that pop up along the way. Here are some ways to help make sure you don't outlive your available assets.

1. Determine Financial Readiness

Sometime before making the final decision to retire, you should sit down and work with a professional financial planner to figure out your precise financial readiness for retirement. There are more than a few free calculators and other programs available through the internet to help provide a basic assessment of retirement readiness, they frequently do not include all of the important factors and are, at best, a rough indicator. On our site, www.mahoneygps.com, there are number of easy calculators you can use. A professional and experienced financial planner can give you a full assessment of your readiness, and make sure that all the factors that will affect you have been considered. A financial planner can help turn your retirement from a dream to a realistic goal with a plan to get there, moving you closer to a secure retirement by making use of what you have already

saved and what you will be able to save and invest before
and after retirement.

2. Look Into Adding Annuities To Your Financial Portfolio

Gaining an above-average rate of return can be lucrative
and is often the reason why investors take risks on their
investments. However, a retiree-investor cannot take risks
like a younger trader with employment and stable income.
Retiree-investors may be more interested in safer options for
investment, like annuities. However, not all annuities are the
same. To choose the right kind of annuity to invest in, decide
what your goal is and select the option that fits your situation
best. The table below covers the general features of
annuities.

General Features	Fixed Annuity	Variable Annuity
Guaranteed Principal: Cannot lose the initial capital, regardless of the subsequent performance of the investment.	√	-
The principal and the return are not guaranteed.	-	√
Guaranteed earnings at fixed rate of interest, or a fixed amount through a fixed period. (Certain programs may pay interest as well as minimum guaranteed amounts.)	√	-
Investment is in funds with specific investment objectives. Payments to you are decided by the fund's performance. Fund usually (but not always) is made up of a mix of bonds, money markets and stocks.	-	√
Equity Indexed: Where the value of the annuity is determined by the performance of the selected stock index.	√	-

Market Value Adjusted: Annuities in which you are usually allowed to choose both period of investment and rate of return within the pre-established limits. You may or may not be permitted to make withdrawals before the investment period has ended.	√	-
Deferred Annuity: A type of annuity meant as deferred income, to be used for future savings and investing. Can be purchased with a lump sum or through several deposits. Appropriate for retirement planning if you have a somewhat longer period available before retirement.	√	-
Immediate Annuity: Pays income immediately after purchasing the annuity. Usually purchased with a single lump sum payment. Appropriate if you are already retired, or near retirement. Turns a lump sum into an income stream.	√	√
Fixed/Guaranteed Period: The annuity is pre-arranged to make payments for a certain number of years. Should you die before the annuity expires, your beneficiaries will receive the remaining payments.	√	√
Lifetime Annuity: Payments continue for the rest of your life and end on your death.	√	√
Joint and Survivor Annuities: These are paid to you for as long as you live. On your death they continue to be paid to a beneficiary, usually your spouse, for as long as he or she lives	√	√
Qualified: Can be purchased using assets from retirement plans such as 403(b) accounts or IRAs.	√	√
Nonqualified: Can be purchased using after-tax funds held outside of a retirement plan.	√	√
Flexible Premium	√	√
Single Premium	√	√
Regulation through state insurance departments	√	√
Regulation through Federal Securities and Exchange Commission	-	√

There are some combination annuities that combine features of both fixed and variable. A number of annuity companies have riders such as guarantee income for life. This vehicle is popular for near retirement and retirees.

An Equity-Indexed Annuity is a contract with an insurance or annuity company. The word *equity,* which was previously tied to indexed annuities, has been removed to help prevent the assumption of stock market vesting being present in these products. This type of tax-deferred annuity, whose credited interest is linked to an equity index — typically the S&P 500 or international index — guarantees a minimum interest rate (typically between 1% and 3%) if held to the end of the surrender term and protects against a loss of principal. Although the returns may be higher than fixed instruments such as CDs, money market accounts, and bonds, they are typically not as high as market returns. Equity Index Annuities are insured by the State Guarantee Fund which is similar to the insurance provided by the FDIC. The guarantees in the contract are backed by the relative strength of the insurer.

Contracts, such as these, may be suitable for a portion of the assets held in a portfolio for those who want to avoid risk and are in retirement or nearing retirement age. The objective is to realize greater gains than those provided by CDs, money markets or bonds, while still protecting principal. The long term ability of Equity Index Annuities to actually beat the returns of other fixed instruments is debatable.

Equity-Indexed Annuities may also be referred to as Fixed Indexed Annuities or Simple Indexed Annuities. Again, the mechanics of these annuities are often complex and the returns can vary greatly depending on the month and year the annuity is purchased. Remember, most annuities also incur surrender charges for early withdrawal.

These are only the general features of annuities. Annuities can often be customized to include several of these features. As an example, a variable annuity could also have a fixed component to ensure that you retain at least part of your principal and ensure some guaranteed return on the investment. It's important to ask your provider what benefits and features are available.

Remember; don't be afraid to ask a professional financial planner to help you decide if an annuity is right for you, and what type and features you should opt for.

3. Decide When To Start Drawing On Social Security

The income you receive from Social Security will take some of the financial load off your savings and investments during your retirement years. You have the option of when to decide to begin receiving Social Security checks, and it is important to choose the right time to do so.

Here's why:

- It's possible to begin to receive your Social Security benefits as early as age 62. However, doing so will permanently reduce the benefits for which you are eligible. If for example you turned 62 by 2011 and you then began drawing social security, the reduction will have been nearly 30%.

- Additionally, if you choose to receive your Social Security benefits prior to the beginning of the year in which you reach retirement age, the paid benefits are reduced by $1 for each $2 you earn past the annual limit. For 2010/2011, the annual limit was $14,160.

- Once you reach the *year* at which you reach retirement age, your benefit payments are reduced by $1 for every $3 earned above the limit for the year (For 2010/2011: $37,680). However, the Social Security Administration only factors in earnings from before the month in which you reach full retirement age.

- Starting the month you reach retirement age, you are permitted to receive benefits without reductions.

As a result, unless you have no other choice but to begin drawing on the money, it is better to leave drawing on your Social Security benefits until after you have reached retirement age.

Pension Annuity Payments vs. Lump Sums

When distributing benefits, a significant portion of defined-benefit plans (as well as target-benefit and money-purchase based pension plans) will offer the employees a choice between two options: an annuity or a lump sum. If you are asked to choose, it is best to consult with your financial planner before making a final decision. Your financial planner will be able to look at your other assets and tell you whether it is more beneficial in your case to take a guaranteed income stream (which can be transferred to your spouse in the event that you die before him or her), or whether you would be better off taking the lump sum and reinvesting it.

4. Working Retirement Is An Option

Just because you have reached retirement age does not mean you *must* stop working. If you enjoy your job and are still in good health, what's to stop you from working past the expected retirement age? The benefits of a working retirement include a steady income stream, as well as other benefits offered by employers to employees, potentially including medical and dental insurance, which can save you the money you would otherwise have spent without insurance.

5. Spend Wisely

The ideal retirement is one where you can enjoy life to its fullest without having to spend too much time worrying about the state of your finances. A budget can help you achieve this idea. Budgeting is a very basic and completely vital part of planning your finances. It allows you to determine what kind of lifestyle you will be able to afford, and to continue to afford in the future. Once you have budgeted for necessities and fixed costs, you can use what is left over to budget your disposable income. There are a great many discount and reward programs available for seniors – many stores, restaurants and even movie theaters offer discounts to people over 65. Check online, as many of the available discounts will be advertised somewhere on company websites. And if you don't know if a business offers any seniors discounts, don't be afraid to ask. The money you can save through careful budgeting and taking advantage of senior discounts can add up and help your retirement fund stretch even further.

This is not pinching pennies and doing it does not make you a cheapskate. It makes you thrifty and financially savvy. A little careful planning and research can let you do all the things you love at a much lower cost.

6. Consider a Reverse Mortgage

Reverse mortgages were once a scary proposition, but since 1991, the HECM (Home Equity Conversion Mortgage) reverse mortgage, insured by FHA/HUD, have been a safe and tax free way of making one's retirement dollars stretch.

Homeowners who want to remain in their home can access their equity with no income or credit score qualifications. The only requirements are that all borrowers must be at least 62 years old at closing, the home be must be a primary residence and must meet all FHA minimum standards. Reverse mortgage are mortgages, but borrowers do not have to repay this loan as long as they reside in the home. You can receive the available equity as a lump sum, in monthly payments or use it like a line of credit that has guaranteed growth. Some borrowers use a combination of these options. Borrowers are responsible for real estate taxes, insurance and maintenance. FHA/HUD will insure loans on single to four family homes, condo's in FHA approved condominium projects and PUD's. Again, borrowers must reside in the premises and the loan must be repaid when the borrowers permanently vacate the home. However, there is no personal liability and no other assets can be attached to repay the loan. The most that can ever be owed is the housel

Some financial advisers are currently utilizing reverse mortgage lines of credit as a strategic source of income for clients who rely on their investments for retirement income. If their investments do not produce the income needed in any one period, instead of selling off securities, they use the line of credit to supplement their income. When the market performs well, the funds borrowed can be repaid and then the money becomes available to borrow again should they need it. Additionally, any interest paid is tax deductible.

For people who wish to retire early and delay taking social security, a reverse mortgage can provide an additional source of income. Using a reverse mortgage as a tax free source of income is another good strategy.

Conclusion

During your retirement your financial stability will become much more important and much more tenuous, as you will no longer have employment income and will need to rely on your pensions and accumulated savings. Before making the big decision to retire, it is vital to work with a financial planner who can help you form a realistic and effective plan for retirement. Taking care and consulting with a financial professional will help you stretch your resources much farther than you otherwise might have been able to.

4 Ways to Improve
Your Retirement Readiness

Some Americans may be better prepared for retirement than they realize. About 56% of baby boomers and Generation X (people aged between about 38 and 65 now) are saving enough to cover their basic retirement costs, including uninsured medical expenses, according to a recent projection by the Employee Benefit Research Institute, a Washington-based nonprofit think tank.

The bad news is that 44% of these aren't saving enough, and some of those people are on the lowest rungs of the income ladder, so they may have little opportunity to ramp up savings as they age.

Still, while some people face a troubling retirement outlook, others in that 44% group can take steps to get their savings on track.

Some Americans are facing a retirement crisis, but they aren't the majority. For the longest time, studies have always pointed out that about 50% of Americans seem clearly ready for retirement. But it's a mistake to assume that the other half are in deep trouble.

Instead, people fall along a spectrum of retirement readiness, with 20% to 30% of Americans "partially ready" for retirement. A significant number of people can take some steps between now and retirement to move the dial to "prepared".

Here are four ideas to improve your retirement readiness.

1.   *Increase Your Savings Rate 1% or 2% Each Year*

You're tired of being admonished to save more, but why not do it relatively painlessly with a small annual increase? Ramping up your current 5% 401(k) contribution rate to 10% over a four-year period means an extra $550 in monthly income in retirement, according to an analysis by Fidelity Investments. The analysis assumes a 37-year-old worker with a $74,000 annual salary, $20,000 401(k) account balance, 3% employer match, an 8.35% annual return, and a retirement age of 67.

Then consider going beyond 10%. If somebody is going to be saving their entire career, 15% is typically what most financial professionals suggest you put in.

2.   *Work Two Extra Years*

Maybe you're not keen on the new normal for retirement, which for some means not retiring at all. But there is a middle road: Work just two more years than planned.

Consider two hypothetical people, each with $1 million in savings. One retires at age 64, the other at 62. They both seek $75,000 a year in retirement.

For the early retiree, the combination of a lower Social Security payout (about $1,500 monthly versus $1,750 monthly), two fewer years of earnings on his savings, and the portfolio hit from pulling $150,000 out for living expenses in those two years, adds up to him running out of money by age 88.

Solely by virtue of waiting two years, the other retiree has $242,358 in savings at age 90, according to one analyst. The analysis assumes a 6% rate of return, and doesn't take into account taxes, variability of returns, or additional savings from delaying retirement for two years. The Social Security payout estimates are based on his clients' experiences.

3. Buy an Annuity

A major conundrum of retirement planning is estimating how long you will live. Longevity insurance helps savers mitigate the risk of getting that answer wrong -- that is, living longer than expected and running out of money.

For some investors, they like to place the longevity risk on an insurance company. The insurance company provides an investor with a contract of what the benefits will be up until death. This is known as a living benefit.

The idea is that when you retire at, say, 65, you take 10-15% of your savings to buy an annuity that doesn't start paying out until age 85.

The retiree gets to retain control over the bulk of their portfolio, yet also gains insurance to back up their savings in the event of a long life.

You only have to put down a relatively small percentage of your 401(k) or IRA balance to get relatively decent monthly income at that point. That means you can focus on saving for the years up until age 85.

4.   Work Part-Time For Five Years

Getting a part-time job -- if you can find one and your health allows it -- is another way to prime the retirement-savings pump.

Take someone who retires at 65 with a final salary of $75,000. He'll need a total of about $780,600 in retirement savings if he doesn't work part time -- but that drops to $661,000 if he works part time for five years earning 30% of his former salary, according to another analysis.

The analysis assumes a 3% inflation rate, a 5% rate of return and the retiree wanting to replace 85% of pre-retirement income, not having a traditional pension, and dying at age 88.

Using the same assumptions, someone who retires at 65 with a final salary of $50,000 will need a total of $490,000 in retirement savings if they don't work part time, but $411,000 if they work part time for five years earning 30% of their former salary, according to the analysis.

If the part-time job pays 50% of their former salary, the retiree needs total savings of about $358,000, or about $132,000 less.

This would be your 'second act'. If you go this route, you need to choose something you love to do, and get paid as a side benefit.

Generating Income Through Hobbies

Retirement means quitting your job and relaxing all day, and while that is good at first you will quickly find that it's better to have something to fill the time with. If you had a hobby before, perhaps you'll be able to put more time into it. If you didn't, you may find yourself picking up one or two. If you find you enjoy your hobby, it may be possible to make a little money from it. It means a little extra effort, but also a little extra cash that can help to ease financial strains. It doesn't matter what your hobby is, the possibilities are endless. How well you will be able to turn your fun into funds depends mostly on how much time and labor you're willing to dedicate to pursuing it as a business.

If you're having trouble coming up with an idea for turning your pastime into profit, here are a few ideas for adapting hobbies into post-retirement businesses.

Sales:

Online Auctions

If you've got enough of a collection of things, like old records, toys, or vintage clothing that you are looking to get rid of, an online auction can be a step up from the old fashioned yard sale. Sites like eBay allow people to search for and bid on exactly the things they want, and collectors often scour the sites and are willing to pay top dollar for anything 'antique'. If you don't already have a collection, it's even possible to turn a profit buying and re-selling items from eBay. If you're an expert on something, or if you're just looking for a little bit of buy/sell risk taking, it's possible to make a tidy sum bidding and re-selling your purchases on other websites for a profit.

Selling and Re-Selling On Amazon

If you have storage space to spare or a large collection of books, records or CD's, it's possible to sell items like these through Amazon.com. If you don't already have a collection, flea markets and thrift stores often have hidden treasures at bargain prices that can be resold for profit. However, you will need to account for shipping costs, and storing and shipping items can be time consuming.

Handmade Arts and Crafts on Etsy

Perhaps you're a crafty person who knits, crochets or sews. If you are, then it's worth looking into Etsy.com. Etsy is an online marketplace for marketing and selling your handmade arts and crafts. If that's what you're good at, you can earn some money by making small crafts and posting them for sale on Etsy.

Sell and Re-Sell At Yard Sales and Flea Markets

If you're not an Internet person, it's more than possible to go about the selling and re-selling of "lost treasures" the old fashioned way – in real life. It can be a fascinating hobby "treasure hunting" through flea markets and yard sales. When you come across bargains, snap them up if you think you can resell them. You can also sell all the same arts, crafts and handmade items at a yard sale just as well as over the Internet.

Teach/Tutor:

This will earn a little more money than a simple hobby, and you can do it on your own schedule as well. You might have some knowledge of math, science, history, or English, and it's possible to offer that knowledge for some income by advertising your services as a tutor, either through a website or through ads and fliers. Outside of 'school subjects' there is always demand for people who can teach a foreign language, or teach non-English speakers how to speak English. Art and music lessons are also always in demand. Remember to consider whether you would rather have students come to you at your home or if you would prefer to meet with them somewhere else.

Try eduFire.com

An interesting new online option for tutoring services has popped up called eduFire.com. This website matches students and tutors over the Internet for one on one learning sessions, or group classes. To use it you will need computer skills and be able to market yourself and your teaching ability.

Write

If you have always been interested in writing, you might try freelancing for a local newspaper or a website that covers one of your interests. Fiction writing is more difficult to get into and frequently less profitable, but if you produce a high volume of work and are dedicated to constantly submitting it to publishers, it's possible to make some money with stories and poetry.

Party Planning

Are you always the one people go to for advice when they're planning an event? It might be because you're good enough at it to turn it into something of a business. Set up a website and some advertising for your services and charge money for that advice.

Organizing

If you enjoy the process of tidying up and organizing your home, that can be the starting point for a business as well, offering your talent for organization to the perpetually disorganized. But be sure you can handle the physical side of the work, as there will always be closets to clear out and stacks of paper to carry.

Gardening and Baking

Farmers' markets and vegetable stands are more and more prevalent nowadays as people seek to buy local and organic foods. If you grow your own fruits and vegetables, or make jams and baked goods, it's worth finding out how much it would cost you to set up a stand at a nearby market.

Searching for Gold

If you live on a coastline and you love the outdoors, you might be interested in obtaining a good metal detector and going "treasure hunting" for real. Beachcombers often find dropped jewelry or old coins, and the prices of precious metals have been climbing steadily, making this a good way to keep active while putting some money in your pocket.

The Most Important Thing

It's good to make some money from your hobby, but the main thing is to keep enjoying your retirement. Remember, you retired so you could stop working and enjoy the rest of your life. If you want to make money without sacrificing your enjoyment of your retirement years, you should do something that you truly enjoy, so that the time you put into it is time spent doing something you want to do.

Just because an insurance company advertises they are the cheapest doesn't make it true. A consumer should review their insurance needs and remarket their insurance every 2 or 3 years. This will insure they are properly covered and are paying a competitive rate for their coverage.

~ Joseph Cantarella, Executive VP, Keep Ins.

Health Care

Your health *will* drive your retirement decisions and options. The older you get, the more likely it becomes that health care will be a major and recurring concern. You need to be very careful when choosing and using health care providers--as well as other people who can make life and death decisions for you, when you can't. You'll want to consider long-term care insurance, Medicare Part B, Medicare Supplemental and Medicare Part D. You may also profit from understanding the various Medicaid tricks, traps, and troubles which have bankrupted many a family when one member needed nursing home care.

What You Need To Know About Health Insurance

With the health care costs continuing to rise, it is important to understand that health insurance is not really an option for most individuals—more like a necessity. While you are working, most employees obtain a health plan from their employer, but once you hit retirement the employer paid premiums, low co-payments, and cheap out-of-pocket expenses may get thrown out their window. Unless your retirement with your employer covers your health insurance after retirement (which most do not) then you need to consider what options of health care coverage are available to you. And choosing the best health insurance policy and coverage takes time to research before you can make a decision on the right plan for you and your needs.

Health Plan Coverage

There are many health plans to choose from and these plans also have many features and exclusions. The older you get, the harder it can be to get health insurance coverage. So keep in mind that the sooner you can establish one after retirement and the healthier you are when you get one, the better off you will be where the costs, terms, and conditions of the policy are concerned.

Types of Coverage

There are five main areas of coverage you need to be concerned with when shopping for a health insurance plan-- major medical coverage, choice of health care providers, lifetime maximum benefits, deductibles and co-payments, and guaranteed renewals.

Major medical coverage is your primary concern because it is the most expensive part of health care that can drain your wallet if you have a major accident or are diagnosed with a major illness. This type of coverage includes hospital stays, visits to the doctor, X-rays, and laboratory work.

The next type of coverage you need to be concerned with is your ability to choose the doctors and specialists you want. While being able to choose any doctor you want should not be the deciding factor for you to choose a health plan, you should be aware of what your patient rights are with the policy. A plan that allows you to choose any doctor may be very expensive—making it cost prohibitive for you to have.

The most common and least expensive of health plans are Health Maintenance Organization (HMO) plans and Preferred Provider Organizations (PPO) plans. Both HMO's and PPO's help to keep the cost of health insurance, co-payments, and out-of-pocket expenses down.

While there are differences between HMO and PPO plans, these plans have more similarities than differences. The main difference between the two plans occurs when the doctor you want to see is not on the preferred provider list. If you have an HMO, it may not cover the cost of services from the doctor. A PPO may still pay the majority of the expenses, and then you are responsible for paying the rest.

The third item you want to be aware of when shopping for a health plan is the lifetime maximum benefits. This is the total amount the insurance will pay over the life of the policy. Ideally, you may want to choose a plan that has a maximum lifetime benefit of $5 million or does not have a maximum limit at all—just in case you have a scenario with a major illness or have a serious accident.

Fourth, you need to consider the deductibles and co-payments involved with the policy. These two items have a direct effect on the premium of the policy, so the higher the amount of the deductible and the higher the amount of the co-payments, the lower the monthly premium payments. The best way to keep your health insurance premiums affordable for you is to choose a plan with the highest deductible and co-payments you can afford.

Finally, you may want to seek a plan that has a guaranteed renewal feature—especially as you get older. This feature allows your policy to continue to renew, unless you cancel it, regardless of your health condition and without having to administer to a physical exam. Again, as we age, our bodies are more susceptible to illness, disease, and complications. We need a policy that sticks by us no matter how healthy we are as we age. The guaranteed renewal feature extends our protection at a time when we probably need it the most.

Purchasing a Plan

So where is the best place for you to buy a health insurance plan? You have several options when shopping for a health insurance provider. First, you can contact health insurance agents, who represent several different health insurance companies who can help you choose from a menu of providers and services for the policy that is right for your needs. You can also go directly to the health insurance providers and shop and compare the policies yourself. Doing it yourself can be time consuming and confusing, if you are not familiar with how insurance policies work. Finally, there are online organizations like the Insurance Information Institute *www.iii.org*, where you can find information on the types of policies that may be available to you and where you may be able to purchase a policy.

If you haven't retired and you have an employer provided health insurance policy, find out if this policy does or can extend into your retirement. If you are self-employed and have insurance coverage, talk with your provider to find out how your retirement and/or closing your business (if applicable) will affect your coverage. If it terminates once you retire (whether employed by a company or self-employed) then your best bet is to research and compare some of the older and larger health insurance companies' policies, which may offer more competitive pricing.

Some health insurance companies require physical exams and look into your medical history, which can cause you to be denied if the insurance company thinks you are too high of a risk. If you are denied insurance coverage contact health insurance companies that do not require a health exam to qualify. Depending on the state where you live, some states offer plans to those who cannot qualify for health coverage any other way.

After Age 65

For those who are already retired or are 65 or older, the government offers a health insurance plan--Medicare.

Medicare has four major parts of enrollment:

1. Part A: Hospital expenses
2. Part B: Physician and other expenses
3. Part C: Supplemental coverage (third party insurer)
4. Part D: Prescription drug coverage

While Part A Medicare coverage is automatic once you apply for Medicare, Parts B, C, and D are optional. With Medicare coverage you are responsible for meeting deductibles and paying co-payments for Medicare services. To bridge the gap there is also Medigap insurance, which may cover the charges Medicare does not. If you cannot afford to pay for the deductible and co-payments because of low income, Medicaid is available to help people in this situation. Medicaid a state funded insurance plan and can also be used with Medigap insurance.

Part D coverage is relatively new, having started in 2006, and helps cover the cost of prescription drugs. However, there are restrictions to the program that you need to know about before opting in, which may only make sense to do if you expect to pay more than $5,000 on prescription drugs in a year.

With Medicare you are responsible for paying the first $3,600 of prescription drug coverage out of your own pocket before Medicare kicks in. Medicare then pays 95% of prescription drug costs after the first $5,100. So unless you pay or expect to pay more than $5,000 on prescriptions, then this may be a coverage you choose not to partake.

There are enrollment restrictions with Part D, so be sure to make an educated decision before opting out. If you choose not to enroll in Part D when you apply for Medicare, but decide to enroll later, there is a penalty fee charged. A better option may be to enroll in the lowest cost Part D option available and then upgrade to a better coverage option later, if necessary, to avoid paying the penalty. For complete Medicare information, *visit www.medicare.gov.*

Long-Term Care Insurance

Once you have your health plan coverage established, you may think the battle is over and sigh in relief. The truth is that many retirees worry whether or not to buy long-term care insurance (LTC), which covers extended stays in nursing homes. These policies are very expensive and have many exclusions and limitations associated with them, which is one reason why the decision to buy or not plagues many people.

There are more reasons not to buy a LTC than there are benefits to buying it. First, the stay in a nursing home for most is less than one year, which means the cost of a policy far exceeds the cost of paying for a one-year stay out your own pocket. Second, if you are covered by Medicare, it picks up the cost for the first 100 days of a stay in a nursing home, as long as certain conditions are met. Finally, most individuals have family or friends who can care for them during this one-year period, which means they avoid the nursing-home stay altogether.

Healthcare for Baby Boomers

The Commonwealth Fund reports that more than 60% of adults aged 50 to 64 who are working (or have a working spouse) have been diagnosed with at least one chronic health condition--arthritis, cancer, diabetes, heart disease, high cholesterol, or high blood pressure. The report goes on to say 1/5 of older workers and their spouses -- 7 million Americans -- either do not have healthcare insurance or have been uninsured at some time since they turned 50. Is U.S. healthcare in trouble for baby boomers?

This report does raise an alarm for how the U.S. healthcare system can cope with the current and growing future needs of aging baby boomer population.

Baby boomers face:
- Increasing healthcare issues
- Unstable healthcare insurance coverage
- High medical costs
- Debt problems

Inadequate Healthcare Coverage

Of those baby boomers who have healthcare coverage, many do not have coverage that is adequate to cover all of their medical expenses.

In fact, approximately 6% of insured older working adults -- 1.8 million people -- are underinsured. Their healthcare plan does not protect them against high medical expenses when compared to their income. The Commonwealth Fund study also found that 1/3 of those surveyed already had medical bill problems or were in medical debt. Approximately 23% said there was a time when they went without. Overall, there is a lack of confidence in healthcare coverage among boomers. Boomers with low to middle-class incomes are worried about being able to afford their healthcare insurance coverage during retirement. With 42% of boomers having incomes between $40,000 and $60,000, they are "very worried" about being able to afford healthcare insurance. A large majority (72%) said they are interested in receiving Medicare before age 65 — if this were a possibility. Even boomers with higher incomes agree that they would be "very or somewhat interested" in early enrollment in Medicare.

Out-of-pocket healthcare expenses seem to be what takes the biggest chunk of household income from boomers when it comes to health care -- with 5-11% or more of their income being spent on out-of-pocket healthcare costs and premiums -- no matter which income bracket they fall into.

Self-Employed Individuals Face the Biggest Healthcare Burden

The self-employed are the ones that may be the most burdened by the healthcare costs. Close to 55% of self-employed boomers spend more than $3,600 per year on healthcare insurance premiums. For those with individual policies, ¾ of the boomers spend 5% or more of their annual income on premiums and out-of-pocket medical expenses. You can read the full Commonwealth Report on aging boomers online at *www.cmwf.org*.

Can You Afford To Grow Old?

At this point you are probably wondering if you can afford to grow old and retire. It's a valid thought, but since we have no choice in the matter, we have to prepare for these additional expenses. Planning and making some lifestyle changes may be in order to accomplish it and while nothing is guaranteed there are some steps you can take to make sure you can afford to take care of your health and your spouse's health when you retire.

- *Long Term Care Insurance*

Previously, we discussed the reasons why long term care insurance may not be right for everyone, but there are individuals who benefit from buying LTC insurance. The longer you live, the more likely the chance that you will need help with daily living such as bathing, dressing, or preparing meals. And the longer you live, the higher the chances are that your loved ones may go before you do, leaving nobody that can take care of these needs for you. Others do not want to burden their loved ones with taking on these responsibilities. These are all candidates for long term care insurance.

And to add insult to injury none of these activities are covered by Medicare. Medicare also does not pay for nursing home care considered custodial in nature. Again, this is where long term care insurance comes to the rescue.

- *Secondary Health Insurance*

Supplementing your Medicare benefits may be necessary to ensure that you are covered once you retire. Check with your employer before you retire to see if you are eligible for health care benefits during retirement—these benefits act as a secondary or supplemental insurance to Medicare, helping to cover the large annual Medicare deductible and the 20% co-payments.

- *Medicare Supplements*

There are health policies specifically designed to supplement Medicare coverage if you are not covered by your employer's policy after retirement. The benefit levels and costs of these policies vary, but it can help to curb healthcare costs.

- *Save On Prescriptions*

When feasible, shop and compare your prescription drugs. Talk to your doctor before he writes the prescription to see if there is a generic version of the medication—helping you to stretch your retirement dollars and save money on your medications. Find pharmacies and programs offering discounts to seniors like the AARP mail order drug program. Some seniors report savings of up to 50% on prescriptions.

- *Preventative Care*

The best way to save on your healthcare costs is to live a healthy life and save medical costs altogether. Illnesses like diabetes and heart disease can kill a lot of healthcare dollars over your lifetime. Exercise, eat a healthy diet, don't smoke and drink alcohol in moderation. Do what you can to prevent health problems down the road.

Research Your Medicare Options Before Retirement

All of the problems that healthcare can cause during retirement is the number one reason why you should research your Medicare options before you retire. Then you will know if Medicare fits your needs on its own or if you have to supplement it with another type of coverage. Part of planning your investment portfolio for retirement includes healthcare coverage.

Why Should You Research Medicare Now?

While Medicare does cover many basic medical expenses, it does not cover all of your medical expenses during retirement. There are also many exceptions and limitations of Medicare. This is why it important to understand all of the coverage, deductibles, co-payments, and limitations of Medicare now so that you can obtain supplemental health care insurance that will cover the rest of your health benefits. Also, it is easier and less expensive to get insurance when you are younger and healthy, so do your research as far in advance as you can so you can adequately plan for all aspects of your retirement.

Make sure that part of your financial investment portfolio is devoted to covering medical expenses during retirement. Having the knowledge of what Medicare has to offer and where it falls short gives you the power to make decisions that will get you through your golden years.

Facts and Fiction About Long Term Care (LTC)

Few people understand the risks, costs, and options associated with long term care. And why would they? It's not pleasant to consider the possibility that you could spend the end of life unable to care for yourself. But it's also unpleasant to confront the reality that if one spouse needs long term care, it could consume those hard earned assets the other needs for living expenses.

Roughly 40% of deaths in the United States are now preceded by a period of enfeeblement, debility, or dementia that can last for years. Studies put the chances of a 65 year old eventually needing long-term care at 20% to 49%.

But Medicare covers only the first 20 days of skilled nursing care when physician ordered treatment occurs within 30 days of a three–day hospital stay. For days 21 to 100, the patient is responsible for the first $128 per day (in 2008), and all costs beginning on day 101.

Three Levels of Long Term Care

1. Custodial care is primarily for people who need help with the six basic activities of daily living — eating, dressing, walking, getting in and out of bed, taking medicine, and bathing. Medicare does not cover this type of care.

2. Intermediate care is for people who require occasional nursing care or rehabilitative care by trained medical professionals. Some people can receive this care at home,

while others may need to be in a nursing home. Medicare may cover some types of intermediate care, subject to the limits mentioned above.

3. Skilled nursing care is for people who no longer need to stay in the hospital but who require the direct daily care of doctors, nurses, and other health–care professionals. This type of care exceeds the "helping hands" assistance that family members are capable of giving.

When Medicare will not help, many people think that Medicaid will pick up the slack. While Medicaid might cover long term care expenses, it generally won't kick in unless you're impoverished ... or until you've "spent down" your assets to the level required in your state. When you apply, Medicaid has the right to look back at all your financial transactions over the preceding 60 months to discover whether you gave away your assets or sold them for less than fair market value to qualify for benefits. If so, you could be ineligible for full Medicaid benefits for up to 100 months.

You may believe that long term care insurance is too expensive, but not having it can be much more expensive if you eventually need care. The national average cost for nursing home care is $70,912 per year, although the cost can vary greatly among geographical regions. By comparison, the national average long term care insurance premium for a 55 year old is about $665 per year for a married individual and $1,075 for a single individual. Waiting until age 65 to purchase a policy would increase these average amounts to $1,292 and $1,923 per year, respectively. These premiums amounts would translate to an average benefit of about $100 per day for three years for married payers and about $150 per day for three years for single payers. (Again, these are national averages. Actual rates will vary widely.)

Ultimately, your decision boils down to paying long term care costs yourself or transferring some of the financial risk to an insurance company through a long term care policy. Choosing the long term care insurance policy that's appropriate for you involves a number of variables, including your age, health, and financial status. By understanding all your options, you'll be better equipped to make an informed decision regarding your long term care needs.

Gifts of Love: Avoiding Probate & Estate Taxes

'Probate issues are minimized when solid estate planning tools have been put in place. Without effective planning and appropriate defensive strategies, issues and disputes can multiply after death. When even the best efforts cannot completely eliminate outrageous allegations of undue influence, incompetency or fraud, estate and probate lawyers protect your rights.
~ John Chakan, Esq.

Why it is better to give, than have it taken away! Why you need a will, why you want to make sure yours never sees the light of day, and how you can minimize your estate's expenses. Avoiding probate and estate taxes with living trusts, life insurance trusts, and irrevocable trusts. Naming executors and guardians. And, most important: debunking the myths surrounding estate taxes and gift giving.

More often than not, couples share joint accounts to take advantage of martial deductions, and to help avoid probate delays and costs. Sometimes joint accounts are a great tool, but sometimes they are not.

These gifts include: clear instructions for your funeral, lists of important names, numbers, and locations, complete account information, gifts to charity, and organized closets.

Knowing that you've planned for the end can ease your burden in the present. Hence the following suggestions for planning a fine finale -- one that has all of your last wishes honored. Taking control of your finances shouldn't end when you do.

Here's what to do:

- First, cover the basics. Make sure your family will have enough ready cash available for at least a few months of living expenses.
- Get your papers in order. Sooner or later, somebody will have to do it. Make it easy on your family, by taking care of it now. Search out all your important records. Put together a chart showing what you have and where everything can be found. (Yeah, it's boring. Do it anyway! It will be so much harder for someone else.)

- You want to make sure that your will, insurance policies, funeral preferences, and living will (if you want no heroics) -- can be easily located when needed. (They should not be in a safe deposit box!)

- Add up your assets and liabilities. Twice. Once for everything you own and owe now. Then a second time, including any pension money or insurance proceeds that your family would receive upon your demise.

- Important: While it's not a light and lively subject, dying may be the most expensive thing you ever do! It's well worth the time and money to make sure you make the most of what you've earned and own. While you and your heirs ought to pay your fair share, you surely don't want your family to pay a penny more in state or federal estate taxes than is required. Right?

- So do your homework. The more estate law basics you know, the more your heirs will receive.

What is Probate?

When someone dies and there isn't a will, probate is the process the court goes through to locate the decedents' assets, determine the value of the assets, and pay the decedent's final bills and estate taxes (if required). Then the court distributes any assets left to the decedent's heirs.

Probate laws vary by state, but general probate steps include:

1. Appointing a personal representative, also called an executor or administrator, to oversee the disposition of the estate.

2. Locating and protecting all of the decedent's assets.

3. Figuring out the date of death values for all of the decedent's assets.

4. Locating all of the decedent's creditors and notifying them of the decedent's death.

5. Publishing a notice in a local newspaper to notify unknown creditors of the decedent's death.

6. Paying all of the decedent's final bills.

7. Filing the decedent's final income tax return.

8. Determining if any state and federal estate tax will be due.

9. If any estate taxes are due, raising the cash necessary to pay the taxes and then paying them in a timely manner.

10. Distributing the balance of what's left of the decedent's assets to the beneficiaries of the estate.

A common and simple way to avoid putting your heirs through the probate process is to establish and fund a revocable living trust.

Setting up a Revocable Living Trust

A revocable living trust is established in writing and involves the Trustmaker, the Trustee, and the Beneficiary. In a typical situation, when the trust agreement is created these three players will be the same person. Once the trust agreement is signed, the Trustmaker funds the trust with his or her assets, then designating the trust itself as the beneficiary of retirement accounts, life insurance, annuities, and any other assets. The Trustee then manages, invests, and spends the trust property for the benefit of the beneficiary.

How a Revocable Living Trust Avoids Probate

Because the Trustmaker doesn't own any of the trust property in his or her individual name—assets are owned by the Trustee for the benefit of the Beneficiary--when the Trustmaker dies, the trust assets do not need to be probated. Even though the Trustmaker has died, the trust itself continues to live on and the Successor Trustee, who is named in the trust agreement now, has the legal authority to step into the Trustmaker's shoes. The Successor Trustee will collect life insurance proceeds, retirement accounts, annuities, and other assets. He or she then pays all of the Trustmaker's final bills, debts and taxes, and then distributes the balance of the trust funds to the Trustmaker's ultimate beneficiaries—also named in the trust agreement.

Taxes

There are four types of taxes you need to be aware of when putting together your estate plan.

- Gift taxes
- Estate taxes
- Generation skipping taxes
- Income taxes

Gift Taxes

As of 2007, the IRS' federal tax code permits you to gift up to $12,000 per year, per person. If you gift more than $12,000 in a year to one person, you are responsible for paying a gift tax on the money you have gifted. This doesn't mean you have to whip out your checkbook and write the IRS a check right away. The federal tax code gives you a lifetime exemption of $1,000,000 to offset your taxable gifts.

For example, your daughter and son-in-law are buying a house, so you give them $100,000 as part of the down payment. For gift tax purposes, the first $12,000 is exempt, but the next $88,000 is considered a taxable gift. This deducts from the $1,000,000 lifetime exemption, leaving you with a new lifetime exemption amount of $912,000.

In addition to the federal gift tax, many states have a state gift tax code, so check with your state for its rules on gift taxes.

Estate Taxes

Federal estate tax apply to estates valued at more than $2,000,000 and is scheduled to increase to $3,500,000 in 2009. In 2010, the estate tax will disappear for the year and decrease to a $1,000,000 limit.

Many states also have an estate tax. Since state laws change frequently, you should consult a qualified estate planning attorney for more information.

Generation Skipping Taxes

A generation skip occurs when you gift or transfer money to someone in your family who is two or more generations below your generation. So you could gift to a child or a grandchild, for example, and skip the taxes. The current federal generation skipping tax allows for transfers up to $2,000,000. You can also transfer assets to a non-relative who is 37 ½ years younger than you.

Some states impose a separate state generation skipping tax. It is best to consult with a qualified estate planning attorney to determine if your state has its own generation skipping tax.

Income Taxes

While many estates and trusts are not affected by gift, estate, or generation skipping taxes the majority of estates and trusts are affected by income taxes. Trust assets continue to earn interest until the assets are distributed and accounts like IRAs, 401ks, and annuities have income tax consequences when the owner dies.

Estates up to $2,000,000 are currently exempt from federal income taxes. Many states impose taxes on the assets owned by residents of their states and real estate owned by non-residents. If an estate exceeds the federal or state limits, then there are a few ways to reduce estate values to reduce the amount of taxes imposed.

1. Reduce Assets

The quickest and easiest way to reduce the value of an estate is to reduce the amount of its assets. The problem is to know how much to spend while still having enough money to get through retirement without running out of money.

2. Gift Assets

You can also gift your assets to friends, family, and charity. Gifting assets have the same problem as spending or reducing assets has, which is knowing how much to spend and while still having enough money to get through retirement without running out of money.

3. Create An Estate Plan

Putting an estate plan in place can drastically reduce and even eliminate estate taxes. Married couples can use a basic AB Trust to significantly reduce or even eliminate estate taxes assessed against their estates. Married couples and individuals can use an Irrevocable Life Insurance Trust (ILIT) to hold and own life insurance.

An ILIT Offers Three Benefits:

1. It deducts the value of life insurance policies from the value of the estate.

2. The insurance proceeds can be used to pay bills, expenses, and taxes.

3. Use advanced estate planning techniques.

There are many other advanced gifting and estate planning techniques designed to reduce or eliminate estate tax. Charitable Remainder Unitrusts, for example, allow the Trustmaker to receive a charitable income tax deduction when the trust is funded. This type of trust also gives the Trustmaker's estate an extra estate tax charitable deduction for the property going to charity after he or she dies.

You have worked very hard for your money and if you want to pass this money on to your children and grandchildren, the last thing you want to do is to burden them with the tax consequences that sometimes come along with this type of income. There is one other tax-cutting measure you can take to gift the money to your children and grandchildren without causing them to suffer the consequences.

Custodial Accounts

Most banks, brokerage and financial institutions have custodial accounts without fees. Depending on the state that you live in, these accounts may be called UTMA's or UGMA's. Since the income received from these types of accounts is taxed at the tax bracket of the child or grandchild, instead of you as the grantor, then less tax will have to be paid on the money.

Projections Are the Key to Your Success

One of the most important things you can do when planning for retirement is a projection. The reason I refer to it as a GPS for your retirement is because it will take you from where you are now to where you want to be in retirement. If you are trying to go somewhere you've never been to before, you need a map...a GPS. Of course the map, in this case, is a projection. There's no short cut to that. You can conceptualize what you want your retirement to look like as you did in the earlier chapters, the lifestyle and so forth, but if you want to know right now where you are, whether you need to work longer or whether you can retire sooner, you need a projection.

The key to retirement planning, I believe, has to do with projections. Once you identify what your expenses will be, you need to identify the sources of income that you will have to meet those needs (Social Security, pensions, investment income, etc.). Say you need $60,000 a year and you will be getting $20,000 of that from Social Security, perhaps a pension of $20,000 and income from your retirement accounts will provide another $20,000. Now you have a plan – a plan to provide enough income to meet your needs.

A lot of people make investment decisions by selecting a stock they heard about from Uncle Joe or investing in a mutual fund they read about. But the real key to retirement planning goes much deeper than that. I believe that a financial projection will guide to your optimum retirement, just like a GPS guides you to your ultimate destination.

Once you have a projection prepared, it is important to review it annually to adjust for any changes that may have occurred in your life. Did your income increase? Have you experienced rising expenses? Is your mortgage paid off? How about your debt? Has that changed? All these things need to be addressed. Any changes will require an adjustment or recalculation of your plan. I don't believe there is any shortcut to successful retirement planning. If you take the time to get on course and adjust for changes along the way, you will transition into the retirement you have envisioned.

Companion to the Book

Studies have shown that writing out goals and/or dreams increases the probability that they will be fulfilled. This workbook was created as a tool to help you define your retirement goals. It contains questions that will get you thinking about what you want to achieve in retirement. Some people want to travel the world. Others are looking forward to spending more time with loved ones. Maybe you are looking to do both! Whatever you envision for your retirement, this workbook will help you.

Sometimes, people feel unsatisfied in retirement because they don't have goals or a passion or something to wake up to every morning. Hopefully this companion will assist you in identifying your goals. As with the projection, your goals should be reviewed periodically to account for any life changes.

The questions contained in this workbook are a compilation of the questions my clients have asked me over the years. You may have questions of your own that may not have been addressed. I have provided space in the back of this workbook for you to write those down. Hopefully these questions will help you identify what is important to you.

I hope that this workbook enables you to develop a clear picture of how you plan to transition from pre-retirement to retirement so that this new chapter of your life is as rewarding and gratifying as you imagined.

Sources for Market News and Insights

Websites: Here are a number of favorites I have on my computer for the markets…in no particular order:

www.thesmartinvestor - okay, there is a particular order for this one … I maintain this site for updated articles, blogs, and financial calculators for clients and prospective clients of Mahoney Asset Management.

www.morningstar.com I have been using this site for over 20 years as a professional resource. They are known for their rating system 5 stars to 1 star.

www.trimtabs.com - as discussed in this book.

www.chartpattern.com - This site focuses on technical of price and volume.

www.finance.yahoo.com

www.google.com/finance

www.realmoney.com I read this throughout the day as they have over 100 experts that blog and twitter with them, including Jim Crammer, who owns the site.

www.pageonefinancial.com   They have a good track record of monitoring asset allocation during volatile markets.

www.corestates.us   William Spiropoulos, CEO appears regularly on CNBC. He called the market bottom in March of 2009.

Newspaper Publications

Investor's Business Daily - is a newspaper I have been reading for over 20 years. It is laid out very well and identifies today's leading companies with a ranking system.

Barrons - I get this newspaper every Saturday.

New York Times – Business section (Week-end delivery)

Sources for Lifestyle

These are some that are on my favorites

VRBO.com - We have used this site for vacation rentals in the summer, and ski season instead of owning a vacation home. Users have reviews and have been reliable.

DrWayneDyer.com - My favorite author. He has written dozens of book on ideas to have a more fulfilled life. The site has articles and blogs. I read it daily for inspiration.

Lohud.com - Find out what is going on local in the Hudson Valley.

Whud.com – Also a great source for news and weather. We look at the calendar of events often.

Amazon.com - I rarely shop in malls. I have bought everything from A-Z from Amazon and have always been 100% satisfied.

Hotels.com - Great deals...when I travel for business I usually get 1/3 off from this site and they have lots of choices.

Jetblue.com - I like traveling from Westchester when I can. Jet Blue seems to be always on time and better service should something go wrong (unlike the big carriers).

Fodors.com - When traveling, this site's a must. It provides information on sightseeing, restaurants and more.

Zagat.com - I have been getting their books now for over 10 years. Great to read other users ratings of decor, food and service, and they are always accurate.

Flickr.com - Great site for sharing pictures. The creativity of the users amazes me. Type in a place you want to see, say Rome, and you can look at all the users' pictures who have been to Rome.

Picasso.com - We have all our photos here. Easy to label, store, share and edit.

iPad - I have the iPad with me constantly. It's easy to use and the apps are amazing.

Google Books is great to preview books before you buy them, or it can be used a reference.

Appendix A: Investment Glossary

A

Accumulation

This is another way of saying: professional buying. A stock is under accumulation when volume expands on days when price moves up.

Alpha

Alpha measures a stock's average monthly move over the past 12 months if the S&P 500 index is unchanged during this 12-month period. For example, a stock with a high alpha of 7 would be expected to rise 7% in a month given an unchanged S&P 500 index.

American Depositary Receipt

Known as ADR's, these securities are created by a U.S. bank and represent foreign securities that trade in the U.S. financial markets.

Annual Report

Companies send their shareholders an annual report at the end of a fiscal year. The magazine or brochure sizes up company operations and displays earnings, sales, balance sheets, and financial footnotes.

Arbitrage

Arbitrageurs make their living by seizing on price differences for a security traded on a different market or in a different form, such as an option or a futures contract. Someone who buys, say, a soybean contract on one market and sells a soybean contract on another exchange is practicing arbitrage by locking in a profit.

Ask
This is the quoted ask, or the lowest price an investor will accept to sell a stock. Practically speaking, this is the quoted offer at which an investor can buy shares of stock.

B

Balanced Mutual Fund
This is a fund that buys common stock, preferred stock and bonds.

Basic Earnings
A simple calculation that takes net income divided by shares outstanding to get per-share earnings.

Basis Point
In the bond market, the smallest measure used for quoting yields is a basis point. One basis point is 0.01 percent of a bond's yield. Basis points also are used for interest rates. An interest rate of 5 percent is 50 basis points greater than an interest rate of 4.5 percent.

Bellwether Stock
The stock of a company recognized as a leader in its industry. For example, IBM is considered a bellwether stock in the computer field. Often, the fortunes of an industry are reflected in the behavior of its bellwether stocks.

Beta

This measures the volatility of a share of stock. A high beta stock, for example, will raise more in value than the stock market average on a day when shares in general are rising. And it will fall more sharply than the average on a day when shares are falling. The Standard & Poor's 500 Index of stocks, an index that represents large-company stocks, has a beta of 1.

Bid

This is the quoted bid, or the highest price an investor is willing to pay to buy a security. Practically speaking, this is the available price at which an investor can sell shares of stock.

Bond

Bonds are debt and are issued for a period of more than one year. The U.S. Government, local governments, water district companies and many other types of institutions sell bonds. When an investor buys bonds, he or she is lending money. The seller of the bond agrees to repay the principal amount of the loan at a specified time. Interest-bearing bonds pay interest periodically.

Book to Bill

Book to bill is the semiconductor book to bill ratio. It reports on the amount of semiconductor chips that are booked for delivery as compared with those that companies already have billed for.

Book Value
A company's book value is total assets minus intangible assets and liabilities such as debt. Book value might be more or less than the market value of the company.

Breadth
This is one of those technical terms you hear in a trading room. It simply demonstrates how broadly a market is moving. When three-quarters of the stocks on the New York Stock Exchange, for example, rise during a given day, an observer might say the stock market had a good breadth. Often, observers will measure the number of stocks advancing against the number declining as one way of monitoring breadth.

Buy Price
Enter here the price you paid for a security. If, for example, you paid 8 1/4 a share for a security, enter 8 1/4.

C

Call option
This security gives investors the right to buy a security at a fixed price within a given time frame. An investor, for example, might wish to have the right to buy shares of a stock at a certain price by a certain time in order to protect, or hedge, an existing investment.

Certificate of Deposit
CDs, as they are called, pay interest to investors for as long as five years.

Change

This shows the change in price of a security from the previous day's closing price. For instance, -1 1/8 means the security has fallen $1.12.

Chief Operating Officer (COO)

A person who has full operational responsibilities for the day-to-day activities of an organization.

Closed-End Fund

A closed-end fund sells a fixed number of shares to investors. Those shares sell on an exchange and vary in price, depending on demand for the fund. A fund's shares, for example, can trade below their net asset value or above their net asset value - depending on investors' demand for the shares. Country funds That represent shares in a specific country or region, such as Italy or France, are often closed-end funds.

Commission

This is a fee an investor pays a broker for buying or selling securities.

Commodity

A commodity is food, a metal or another physical substance that investors buy or sell, usually via futures contracts.

Common Shares

These are securities that represent equity ownership in a company. Common shares let an investor vote on such matters as the election of directors. They also give the holder a share in a company's profits via dividend payments or the capital appreciation of the security.

Consumer Price Index
The CPI, as it is called, measures the prices of consumer goods and services and is a measure of the pace of U.S. inflation. The U.S. Department of Labor publishes the CPI every month.

Consumer Stock
The stock of a company that produces consumer-oriented products like food, beverages, tobacco, pharmaceuticals.

Currency
This shows the currency that a security trades in, such as USD for U.S. dollar.

Current Yield
If a security has a dividend, the yield is the price of a stock dividend. A $10 stock that pays a 50 cent dividend for the year has a 5% yield.

Cyclical Stock
The stock of a company whose fortunes are closely tied to the cyclical ups and downs of the economy in general. For example, General Motors is a cyclical stock since its business of selling autos is highly dependent on a robust economy with its attendant high levels of employment, rising personal incomes, etc.

D

Day High
This is the highest price that a security has traded at during the day.

Day Low
This is the lowest price that a security has traded at during the day.

Devaluation
A lowering of a country's currency relative to gold and/or currencies of other nations. The opposite is revaluation.

Debenture
The common type of bond issued by large, well-established organizations. Holders of debentures representing corporate indebtedness are creditors of the corporation and entitled to payment before shareholders upon dissolution of the corporation.

Convertible Debenture
Corporate securities (preferred shares or bonds) that are exchangeable for a set number of another form at a pre-stated price.

Subordinated Debenture
A debt that is junior in claim on assets to other debt, repayable only after other debts with a higher claim have been satisfied.

Diluted Earnings
A calculation that includes stock options, warrants and convertible securities to get per-share earnings.

Discount Rate
This is the interest rate charged by the U.S. Federal Reserve, the nation's central bank, for loans to member banks. The Fed, as it is called, alters rates to increase or decrease the growth of the nation's economic output.

Distribution
This is another way of saying: professional selling. A stock is under distribution when volume expands on days when price moves down.

Dividend
A dividend is a portion of a company's profit paid to common and preferred shareholders. A stock selling for $20 a share with an annual dividend of $1 a share yields the investor 5 percent.

Dow Jones Industrial Average
This is the best known U.S. index of stocks. It contains 30 stocks that trade on the New York Stock Exchange. The Dow, as it is called, is a barometer of how shares of the largest U.S. companies are performing. There are thousands of investment indexes around the world for stocks, bonds, currencies and commodities.

Duration

A measure of a bond price's sensitivity to a 100-basis point change in interest rates. A duration of 8 would mean that, given a 100-basis point change up/down in rates, a bond's price would move up/down by 8%.

E

Earnings Per Share (EPS)

EPS, as it is called, is a company's profit divided by its number of shares. If a company earned $2 million in one year had 2 million shares of stock outstanding, its EPS would be $1 per share.

Eurodollar

This is an American dollar that has been deposited in a European bank. It got there as a result of payments made to overseas companies for merchandise.

Ex-Dividend

This literally means "without dividend." The buyer of shares when they are quoted ex-dividend is not entitled to receive a declared dividend.

EDGAR

The Securities & Exchange Commission uses Electronic Data Gathering and Retrieval to transmit company documents to investors. Those documents, which are available via DBC's Smart Edgar service, include 10-Qs (quarterly reports), 8-Ks (significant developments such as the sale of a company unit) and 13-Ds (disclosures by parties who own 5% or more of a company's shares).

Exchange

There are three main U.S. Stock exchanges on which securities are traded. AMEX is the American Stock Exchange. NASDAQ is the National Association of Securities Dealers. NYSE is the New York Stock Exchange.

F

52 Week High

This is the highest price that a security has traded at during the last 52 weeks.

52 Week Low

This is the lowest price that a security has traded at during the last 52 weeks.

Federal Funds Rate

This is the interest rate that banks with excess reserves at a Federal Reserve district bank charge other banks that need overnight loans. The Fed Funds rate, as it is called, often points to the direction of U.S. interest rates.

Float

The so-called float is the number of shares of a security that are outstanding and available for trading by the public.

Futures contract

This is an agreement that allows an investor to buy or sell a commodity, like gold or wheat, or a financial instrument, like a currency, at some time in future. A future is part of a class of securities called derivatives, so named because such securities derive their value from the worth of an underlying investment.

G

GAAP (General Accepted Accounting Principles)
Conventions, rules and procedures that define general accounting practice, including broad guidelines and detailed procedures.

Growth stock
The stock of a company whose business is considered recession-resistant and also possesses an above-average growth rate.

H

High price
This is the day's highest price of a security that has changed hands between a buyer and seller.

I

Initial Public Offering
An IPO is stock in a company that is being traded on an exchange for the first time. Investors first read a prospectus that describes the potential of the company and the risks of investing in it.

Insiders
These are directors and senior officers of a corporation -- in effect those who have access to inside information about a company. An insider also is someone who owns more than 10 percent of the voting shares of a company.

J

Junk Bond

A bond with a speculative credit rating of BB or lower is a junk bond. Such bonds offer investors higher yields than bonds of financially sound companies. Two agencies, Standard & Poor's and Moody's Investor Services, provide the rating systems for companies' credit.

K/L

Last

This indicates the most recent trade of a security.

LEAP

A LEAP is a long-term option contract for a company's stock. They usually run for one year or more and are available on several U.S. exchanges.

Limit Order

Investors can place an order to buy or sell securities at a set price. The trade can take place only at that price or a lower one.

Long

Investors who go "long" simply own stock or another security. It is a term that means the opposite of "short," in which investors are short a stock or security because they have borrowed it and sold it to someone else.

Low price

This is the day's lowest price of a security that has changed hands between a buyer and a seller.

M

Margin

This allows investors to buy securities by borrowing money from a broker. The margin is the difference between the market value of a stock and the loan a broker makes.

Market Cap

This is the company's market capitalization. If a company has 10 million shares and the company's shares are selling for $10, the market cap is $100 million.

Market Order

This is an order to buy or sell a security at the current trading price.

Momentum

The rate of acceleration of an economic, price or volume movement. An economy with strong growth that is likely to continue is said to have momentum.

Money Market

Money markets are for borrowing and lending money for three years or less. The securities in a money market can be U.S. government bonds, Treasury Bills and commercial paper from banks and companies.

Money Supply
The stock of money in the economy, consisting of currency in circulation and deposits in checking and savings accounts. M1, M2 and M3 represent money and near-money.

Moving Average
A moving average is an average of a security's price over a specific time period. The average changes, for example, on a 30-day moving average, so that it includes the most current 30 trading days. Moving averages often indicate levels of support or resistance for a security.

Municipal Bond
State or local government offer municipal bonds, as they are called, to pay for special projects such as highways or sewers. The interest that investors receive is exempt from some income taxes.

Mutual fund
Mutual funds are pools of money that are managed by an investment company. They offer investors a variety of goals, depending on the fund and its investment charter. Some funds, for example, seek to generate income on a regular basis. Others seek to preserve an investor's money. Still others seek to invest in companies that are growing at a rapid pace. Funds can impose a sales charge, or load, on investors when they buy or sell shares. Many funds these days are no load and impose no sales charge.

N

Net Asset Value

Listed as NAV in mutual fund listings, net asset value is the market value of a fund's shares. It is calculated at the close of trading.

Net Change

This is the difference between a day's last trade and the previous day's last trade.

Net Profit

This is the difference between the total price you paid for a security, with the brokerage commission you paid, and the current value. It will show either a profit or a loss.

Number of Shares

This is the number of stock shares that a company has outstanding.

Notes

Enter here important notes, such as your reason for buying or selling a security.

NYSE Beta Index

The beta is the covariance of the stock in relation to the rest of the stock market. The Standard & Poor's stock index has a beta coefficient of 1. Any stock with a higher beta is more volatile than the market. Any with a lower beta does the reverse.

O

Open

The price at which a security opens the trading day. Generally, the opening price reflects the previous day's close -- unless extraordinary news or demand to buy or sell have occurred before the market opens.

Open-End Mutual Fund

A fund that sells its shares at net asset value is an open-end fund. It creates shares as investors demand them. Investors buy the shares at their market price. Most mutual funds are open-end funds. Those that aren't are closed-end funds that sell a fixed number of shares to investors.

Open Order

An open order is any order to buy or sell securities that has yet to be executed.

Options

These contracts give the holder the right to buy or sell securities at a set price or a set period of time. Investors often use them to protect, or hedge, an existing investment. An option is part of a class of securities called derivatives, so named because these securities derive their value from the worth of an underlying investment.

Over-the-Counter

The O-T-C market is for securities not listed on a stock exchange.

P

Pay Date
The date on which a declared stock dividend or a bond interest payment is scheduled to be paid.

Percent Change
This calculates the percentage change in the price of a security from the previous trading day's closing price.

Percent Profit
This is your profit or loss expressed as a percentage of your original investment and including the cost of your brokerage commission. If you bought 1,000 shares of a stock at $10, paid a $100 commission and saw the shares rise to $14, your percentage would be 39.6 percent.

Preferred shares
Preferred shares give investors a fixed dividend from the company's earnings. And more importantly: preferred Shareholders get paid before common shareholders.

Premium
This generally refers to extra money an investor is willing to pay to buy or sell something. For a bond, a premium is the amount for which the security sells above its par value. For a stock, a premium is the amount that a security's price exceeds those of its peer group, or comparable stocks.

Previous
This is the closing price of a security from the previous trading day.

Prime Rate
The interest rate banks charge, determined by market forces affecting a bank's cost of funds and the rates the borrowers will accept. This rate tends to become standard for the banking industry when a major bank raises or lowers its rate.

P/E
A stock has a price-to-earnings ratio: the share price divided by earnings per share for the company's most recent four quarters. A projected P/E divides the share price by estimated earnings per share for the coming four quarters.

Put option
This security gives investors the right to sell fixed number of shares at a fixed price within a given time frame. An investor, for example, might wish to have the right to sell shares of a stock at a certain price by a certain time in order to protect, or hedge, an existing investment.

Q/R

Reaction
This term has been around as long as the stock market itself and is used to describe a short-term drop in prices.

Real-time
A real-time stock, bond, option or futures quote is one that reports the most current price available when a security changes hands. A delayed quote shows a security's price 15 minutes and sometimes 20 minutes after a trade takes place.

Record Date
The date on which a shareholder must officially own shares in order to be entitled to a dividend. After the date of record the stock is said to be ex-dividend.

Relative Strength
Stocks which have been strong relative to all other stocks should continue to be relatively stronger in the future and securities which have been relatively weak tend to continue to be weaker.

Return on Equity
Return on equity measures the return, expressed as a percentage, earned on a company's common stock investment for a specific period. It is calculated by common stock equity, or a company's net worth, into net income. The calculation is performed after preferred stock dividends and before common stock dividends. The figure shows investors how well -- how effectively -- their money is being used by managers.

S

Securities & Exchange Commission
The SEC is a federal agency that regulates the U.S. financial markets.

SEC EDGAR
The Securities & Exchange Commission uses Electronic Data Gathering and Retrieval to transmit company documents to investors. Those documents, which are available via DBC's Smart Edgar service, include 10-Qs

(quarterly reports), 8-Ks (significant developments such as the sale of a company unit) and 13-Ds (disclosures by parties who own 5% or more of a company's shares).

Security
This piece of paper proves ownership of stocks, bonds and other investments.

Sell Price
Enter here the price you received when you sold a security. If you received $10 for a share that you sold at 10, then enter 10.

Settlement Date
In U.S. financial markets, an investor must pay for the purchase of shares by the third business day after he or she buys securities. And an investor must deliver an investment that he or she has sold by the third business day after the transaction.

Shareholders' Equity
This is a company's total assets minus total liabilities. A company's net worth is the same thing.

Shares
Enter here the number of shares you own. If you bought shares of a specific security at different times and various prices, enter the total number of shares here and enter the average price for the purchases under Buy Price.

Short Sale

Investors who borrow stock and sell it to someone else are betting the shares go down in price. Then, they can buy back the stock at a lower price and pocket the difference as profit. Going "short" is the opposite of going "long," or owning shares for the long haul.

Short Interest

This is the total number of shares of a security that investors have sold short -- borrowed, then sold in the hope that the security will fall in value. An investor then buys back the shares and pockets the difference as profit.

Special

CBS MarketWatch's portfolio and multiple quote pages offer special buttons that give users the choice to do more research. N = News - This function searches news sources including CBS MarketWatch and Reuters for news pertaining to the ticker symbol selected. S = SEC filings. E = Earnings information from Zacks. H = Hoover's capsules. M = MarketGuide. F = Fundamentals, such as price-earnings ratios and 52-week highs and lows. C = 180 day Chart. FP = Mutual Fund profiles.

Spinoff

A company can create an independent company from an existing part of the company by selling or distributing new shares in the so-called spinoff.

Split

Sometimes, companies split their outstanding shares into larger number of shares. If a company with one million shares did a two-for-one split, the company would have two million shares. An investor, for example, with 100 shares before the split would hold 200 shares after the split. The investor's percentage of equity in the company remains the same.

Spread

This is the gap between bid and ask prices of a stock or other security.

Stock Ticker

This is a lettered symbol assigned to securities and mutual funds that trade on U.S. financial exchanges.

Symbol

This is the ticker symbol of the security. New York Stock Exchange and American Stock Exchange tickers, for example, are three or fewer letters. Example: Ford is F. NASDAQ tickers are four and sometimes five letters. Example: Data Broadcasting Corp. is DBCC. Mutual Fund tickers end with the letter "X." Options tickers have their own help tables.

T

Tick

This refers to a change in the price of a security. An uptick occurs when the last trade in a security takes place at a higher price than the prior trade. A downtick occurs when the last trade in a security takes place at a lower price than the prior trade. An indicator may be fashioned from the difference between the number of NYSE issues showing upticks on the last trade and the number of NYSE issues showing downticks on the last trade. This indicator is known as the TICK, and is found on many quote screens. A TICK of +236 means 236 more NYSE issues last traded on upticks than those trading on downticks.

Trade Sizes

On most trading screens, investors can see the amount of stock available for buyers and sellers. In a stock with a bid price of 18 and an ask price of 18 1/2, for example, a trade size of 10x5 indicates that investors have bids in to buy 10 blocks of 100 shares at the price of 18. Sellers, on the other hand, are willing to sell five blocks of 100 shares at 18 1/2.

Trading Halt

Trading of a stock, bond, option or future contract can be halted by an exchange while news is being broadcast about the security.

Triple-Witching

This occurs on the third Friday of March, June, September and December when futures and stock options, based on the S&P 500 index, all expire on the same day.

Turnover (Securities)

The volume of shares traded as a percentage of total shares listed on an exchange during a period, usually a day or a year. The same ratio is applied to individual securities and the portfolio of individual or institutional investors.

U

U.S. Treasury Bill
U.S. government debt with a maturity that is less than a year is a bill.

U.S. Treasury Bond
U.S. government debt with a maturity of more than 10 years is a bond.

U.S. Treasury Note
U.S. government debt with a maturity of one to 10 years is a note.

V

Value
This is the current price of the security multiplied by the number of shares you own. If you own 1000 shares of Apple Computer, and the shares are selling for $25, the value should be $25,000.

Value Stock
A stock perceived by the marketplace to be undervalued based on criteria such as its price-to-earnings ratio, price-to-book ratio, dividend yield, etc.

Volatility (Historical)
This describes the fluctuations in the price of a stock or other type of security. If the price of a stock is capable of

large swings, the stock has a high volatility. The pricing of options contracts depends in part on volatility. A stock with high volatility, for example, commands higher prices in the options market than one with low volatility. Volatility may be gauged by several measures, one of which involves calculating a security's standard deviation. Stock investors sometimes prefer to measure a stock's volatility versus that of an index, such as the Standard & Poor's 500 Index. This is known as a stock's beta. A beta of 1.2 implies a stock that is 20% more volatile than the S&P 500. When the S&P rises 10%, the stock is expected to rise 12%.

Volume
This is the daily number of shares of a security that changes hands between a buyer and a seller.

W
Warrant
This piece of paper gives an investor the right to purchase securities at a fixed price within a fixed time span. Warrants are like call options, but with much longer time spans -- sometimes years.

X/Y/Z
Zero Coupon Bond
Such a debt security pays an investor no interest. It is sold at a discount to its face price and matures in one year or longer.